SCOTTISH MURDER STORIES

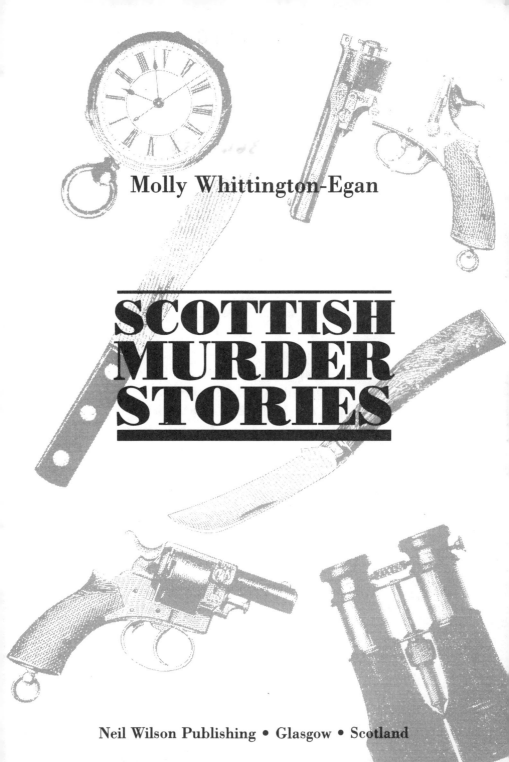

Molly Whittington-Egan

SCOTTISH MURDER STORIES

Neil Wilson Publishing • Glasgow • Scotland

Neil Wilson Publishing
303a The Pentagon Centre
36 Washington Street
GLASGOW
G3 8AZ
Tel: 0141-221-1117
Fax: 0141-221-5363
E-mail: nwp@cqm.co.uk
http://www.nwp.co.uk/

ACKNOWLEDGEMENTS

My special thanks to Stewart Evans,
Robert Gilbert, Melvin Harris,
Dr Marc Hinchliffe, Lewis MacDonald,
Andy Melbourne, Jerry Mullaney and
Richard Whittington-Egan

ISBN 1-897784-80-5
Typeset in Bodoni
Designed by Mark Blackadder
Printed by WSOY, Finland

CONTENTS

INTRODUCTION

I am frequently asked if it is not rather morbid of me to write about the black art of murder. It seems to be considered an unsuitable job for a woman. No-one dares to make the same remark to my august and portly husband, although no doubt where we live in the country it is often thought in private. I am immediately placed in a defensive position by interviewers. That's rich, I think, when the interrogator has come to me fresh from the sight of a serial killer's victim lying on the slab, her liver glistening in a dish, at some post-mortem mocked up on television. That is fiction, as often as not created by the mind of a woman, but such stuff, in my view, is truly morbid, lightly and for a passing thrill to screen an imagined death. Which is not to say that I do not watch it!

Real life crime writers are, in general, quiet, positively reclusive people, leading blameless lives in country cottages. They are not, in general, prone to alcoholism, suicide or aggression. Those in specialized pockets, such as the study of Jack the Ripper, all know one another, which gives a feeling of solidarity, as long as internecine warfare can be avoided. All must have in common a 'knowledge of human nature', be that a truism, based upon past experience. In my case, crime found me, as my husband's expertise in the field gradually influenced me, and my background of English at Cambridge, social work in the old asylums, and my training as a solicitor all came together. You have to go where your know-how lies. Thus anatomized, my motivation can be seen as not morbid but natural.

Morbidity I take to be a nasty preoccupation with unnatural death. A person so afflicted creeps, fancifully, around graveyards at night, sees a *memento mori* in every ambry (the Middle Ages were morbid and with reason) and dwells on horrors. Of all such things I declare myself innocent. In this case, I had the honour of being invited by my publisher, Neil Wilson, to compile a collection of Scottish murder stories of special interest. My intention has been to present the facts of each murder, what exactly happened, and what might have happened. My reader will not be overburdened by lengthy analysis of the consequent trials — this is not the forum for such commentary, although a measure of discussion is sometimes inevitable. Nor have I sought to paint blood: terrible doings speak for themselves.

A first requisite for a selection of this type is a good library and, as ever, my husband, Richard Whittington-Egan, has allowed me full access to his precious volumes, although he will complain that I use his treasures as tools. I fully acknowledge my debt to the old master, William Roughead (1870-1952) Writer to the Signet, but his views are not my views and my images are not his. Writing about murder is a matter of changing taste as well as style. Roughead's mandarin seems old-fashioned, his learning oppressive, but, even so, he stands alone in stature and to those interested I would recommend my husband's biographical and critical study *William Roughead's Chronicles of Murder* (Lochar Publishing, 1991). What is no longer appreciated is Roughead's constitutional irony and his 'high facetiousness', sometimes seen as offensive (although never morbid!). His admiration for 'the attaching [attractive] Lizzie' Borden, or Madeleine Hamilton Smith — 'that tropical and gorgeous flower so astoundingly out of due season' is tongue-in-cheek and not, literally, a celebration of perfidy. He would have run a mile from his 'naughty progeny'.

As for the peculiarly Scottish nature of the stories that

follow, they certainly have their own atmosphere which builds and intensifies in the juxtaposition of seasons and manners. There are special features not intrinsic in plain English crimes, such as the way in which the boots of the murdered man in the Arran case were buried by the local constabulary on the shore below high-water mark in accordance with superstition, to prevent the spirit from 'walking'. Some very strange and mysterious cases are to be found here, such as the riddle of who or what it was that caused Norah Fornario to die naked and alone on a frozen, fairy hill in Iona, frightened out of her wits by black magic. And who can forget the barefoot boys, 11-year-olds, stowaways from Greenock, cast out on the rutted ice-fields to struggle 20 miles to the shores of Newfoundland? I hope that my reader will enjoy these harmless dissections.

CHAPTER 1
THE MISTED MOUNTAIN

The essence of the Arran murder lies (to invoke in one breath the song and Wordsworth's poem) in the conundrum that two men went to climb, went to climb a mountain, one came down and the other stayed up, 'rolled round in earth's diurnal course with rocks, and stones, and trees'.

An act of murder committed high up in the mists so that the island is, as it were, crowned with the old burst of devilry, does produce a special atmosphere. These perceptions are always subjective, but the Isle of Skye, however grand the Cuillins, with their well-remembered peaky silhouette and torrents of scree, seems a kindlier place than the Isle of Arran. Imagine a murder staged under the Cioch, that fine bossed rock, and the whole spirit of the locus would be changed.

Before it happened, just before it happened, an expedition to Arran was, in 1889, the year after Jack the Ripper, a real adventure for a clerkly person from Tooting. Edwin Robert Rose was normally resident in the very stronghold of Pooterdom, deep in the suburbs of south-west London, with their wooded commons and grids of speculative villas.

Here, at Wisset Lodge, Hendham Road, Upper Tooting, with its inspiring view of the red Tudor-style battlements of Springfield, the Surrey County Lunatic Asylum, at the top of the street, Rose lived in comfort and harmony with his father, four sisters and one brother. The mother was missing, presumably dead. Still a bachelor, at 32, he was employed as clerk in the office of James Goodman, builder, of Mostyn Road, Brixton.

He was not at all bad-looking, slight, dark, with deep-set, soulful eyes and a dense moustache. He could have been a doomed young poet of the 1890s, or even, perhaps, the loved special friend of some great Poet Laureate. There was no hint of a girl-friend, and his hobbies were of a manly nature – tennis and cricket, walking and running.

That July, at the start of his fortnight's summer holiday, he booked in first at the Glenburn Hydropathic, in Rothesay, where, by previous arrangement, he joined his friend, the Reverend Gustavus James Goodman, Minister of the Presbyterian Church at Walker-on-Tyne. The cleric was the son of Rose's employer, who, incidentally, knew nothing of the holiday plan. Rose soon made friends with other young men, and, on July 12th, having joined up with a picnic-party from the Hydro, he took the Clyde steamer *Ivanhoe* bound for Arran. He was excited, chatty, approachable, released from the office in Brixton, and stimulated by the sky, and the sea and the impact of the scenery.

The conjuncture of killer with victim is always interesting and sometimes instructive. In this case, the life of the clerk should have been safe enough when he struck up a spontaneous holiday acquaintance with a person of lower social class – a skilled artisan. Victim approached killer on the *Ivanhoe*, mistaking him, it was said, for a member of the picnic-party.

John Watson Laurie – for that was his real name, although he was going under the alias of John Annandale and had a visiting card to prove it – was slightly disreputable, with a touch of 'form' for theft, but not for violence, and his respectable family in Coatbridge were not at all proud of him. On holiday, he was secretive, elusive, determined to conceal the fact that he was a pattern-maker, working at the Atlas Locomotive Works in Springburn, and lodging at 106 North Frederick Street, Glasgow. Snobbery was the background to the unfolding events.

The basically ill-assorted pair got along famously. Rose did most of the talking. Laurie, at 26 somewhat younger than Rose, was fair against the older man's darkness. In physiognomy, he was less refined. Perhaps Rose was drawn to his air of worldliness, a whiff of raffishness, and Laurie appreciated the clerk's touch of class. Rose was a natty dresser, always well turned out for the occasion, and his clothes are a part of the picture. His holiday apparel included a chocolate-brown and white striped tennis jacket, and a white serge yachting cap, rakish beyond the general. Laurie, who could not compete with Rose's finery, was notoriously vain, and the contrast is thought to have irked him. His best effort was a brown knickerbocker suit and stylish stockings.

At this stage, from any normal vantage point, Rose was at risk only of being a victim of theft. The two 'chums' enjoyed their trip to Arran, and arranged to return the following day for a longer stay. It was the Glasgow Fair week and most rooms were taken, but lodgings of a sort had been found by Laurie at Mrs Esther Walker's, in the village of Invercloy, Brodick. A Mrs Shaw had brought him to her. She could offer them a wooden outhouse, a 'lie-to' attached, but with no access to the main house, and with its own door. There was one bed. Very probably they were genuinely lucky to find this roof over their heads and there was no hidden agenda on either side.

Laurie booked to stay from Saturday July 13th, for one week, but Rose was to leave on the following Wednesday. In fact, Laurie sprang Rose on Mrs Walker when he turned up on the Saturday, but she agreed to the terms of 17 shillings for Laurie, and three shillings extra for his friend. Thus discriminated against, Rose was to eat out at Mrs Isabella Wooley's Tea Room, while Laurie was catered for in his own room.

Two other holiday acquaintances, met at the Hydro, and now sleeping, *faute de mieux*, on a friend's yacht in the bay, did not like what they saw of the misalliance. Francis Ord Mickel, a wood-merchant of Linlithgow, and William Thom, a commercial traveller, also of Linlithgow, being Scotsmen will have been quicker to spot that Laurie was not quite the thing, while Rose will have been bamboozled by his accent. Unless, of course, he did not care or rather liked what he intuited.

Anyway, Mickel and Thom were thoroughly suspicious of 'Annandale' and his closely-guarded origins, remarking on his habit of 'coming and going' during a conversation, presumably when the topic was too close to home. Or perhaps he sensed their dislike, and resented their intrusion, and his restless behaviour mirrored his unease. Rose and Laurie announced their intention to climb Goatfell, the highest peak on the island, on Monday July 15th. Laurie had abrogated the role of 'guide'.

Francis Mickel, whose prescience is a curiosity of the events, strongly advised Rose to get rid of his unsuitable companion, even if it meant leaving his lodgings, and he expressly urged him to abandon the plan to climb Goatfell with Laurie. Anxious to please, Rose promised to try, but he obviously did not try very hard, inhibited perhaps by good manners, kindness, or sheer enthusiasm for the project, because when, with Laurie, he saw Mickel and Thom at the pier, he was kitted out from head to foot as a gentleman climber, swathed like a toff in a tailor-made tweed suit with matching tweed cap, leather leggings and leather boots. Ancillary equipment was a waterproof which was black outside and white inside, and naturally he carried a walking-stick.

If Rose had known then that on the Sunday night before, his guide, Laurie, had been seen acting strangely in the lane behind Wooley's Tea Room, he might not have been so confident. The story is that an old Arran woman who lived in one of the cottages nearby watched Laurie walking up and down, talking to himself and looking very odd. 'The De'il's busy with that young chap!' she thought.

Theoretically, this could have been agitation caused by something that had happened, or was about to happen, or it was the outward sign of the hatching of a terrible plan. There is also another factor to take into account: Laurie had toothache.

Unalleviated toothache can affect a man's judgement to a certain level, but not, surely, trigger a homicidal act. We do know that on the Monday, at lunch at 2pm, he complained that he could not eat for toothache. Earlier that morning, he had gone off to get quinine powder as a remedy, but evidently it had not worked.

Laurie was, therefore, a man with toothache as, rather late, soon after 3.30pm, he and Rose set off at a fair pace to climb their mountain. Laurie was the leader, silent with his pain, and, possibly, wicked thoughts. Rose must himself have been uncomfortable in his tweed outfit over brown merino drawers and socks, white linen shirt and white knitted semmit (vest).

At first, after passing through the Castle woods, the foothills to Goatfell were green and mossy moor, the air sultry and buzzing with insects. The terrain was peppered with other holiday-makers (one of them was going at a tremendous rate, trying to break the speed record for the ascent) and seven men in all encountered the couple, one fair, the other dark, as they ascended steadily. The fair one self-contained in front said not a word, but the dark one was happy to exchange pleasantries, as was his disposition.

The climb to the summit at 2,866 feet is a stiff walk by well-defined tracks along the ridges, not a feat of mountaineering, but it is not recommended for those suffering from any degree of vertigo, nor for those sensitive beings who become depressed as they contemplate the insignificance of man against the jagged vastness of nature. The grey granite peaks and deep ravines can make some people long for home.

Surely it was just such a place as this that was in Tennyson's mind when he wrote in *The Passing of Arthur* how Sir Bedivere
'swiftly strode from ridge to ridge'
and
'The bare black cliff clang'd round him, as he based
His feet on juts of slippery crag that rang,
Sharp-smitten with the dint of armed heels.'

Rose and Laurie were last seen at the top around 6pm, standing on a big boulder, apparently discussing and pointing out a different, more difficult route for their descent. Exactly what came next, what was said and done, or done, or merely happened, could have been known only to a golden eagle as it soared.

Three hours later, a shepherd, David McKenzie, sighted Laurie, very tired and on his own, coming down the lonely route of Glen Sannox, but thought no more of it at the time. At about 10pm, Laurie ordered beer and whisky at the Corrie Hotel and said that he was going to walk the six miles to Brodick. He was innocent of bloodstains. The next morning at 11am, Mrs Walker discovered that her two lodgers had disappeared without payment. She had been bilked before, and did not bother to report her loss to the police.

Laurie had, in fact made himself scarce by the early boat, carrying his own yellowish-brown bag, and Rose's black one. Rose was supposed to be on holiday until the 18th, and therefore, at first, he was not missed. Two collie dogs belonging to a farmer named Davidson knew precisely where he lay, but their master did not believe them. When Rose should have alighted from his train in London, fit and hearty after his holiday adventures, his brother, Benjamin, who was there to meet him, was very worried indeed, and the investigation began.

Wet and misty weather defeated search-parties, until a dazzling sun broke through on Sunday August 4th, and a gathering of 200 searchers in divided groups set off at 9am. It was a fisherman from Corrie, Francis Logan, who made the discovery when he tracked an unpleasant smell to a large, granite boulder lying in a gully which led steeply down into Glen Sannox from the ridge of north Goatfell. *Coire-na-fuhren* – Gully of Fire – is the name of the desolate place where they found the remains of the clerk from Tooting. Wedged underneath the boulder and hidden by a man-made constructure of 42 separate stones plugged with heather (for was not Laurie a skilled pattern-maker?) was stretched, face down, fully clothed, the poor, slim body of Edwin Robert Rose. All the pockets of his jacket were empty, and one of them was turned inside out. The skirt of the jacket was turned back over the head, which, with the face, was frightfully smashed, shattered. There was a fracture on the top of the left shoulder blade, and the highest vertebra was lying loose. Strewn higher up the gully without attempt at concealment, possibly in a line of descent, lay Rose's walking-stick, his knife, pencil, and a button and his waterproof, ripped in two parts. His tweed cap *had* been partly hidden, folded into four and flattened beneath a sizeable stone in the stream which trickled down the ravine.

'John Annandale' was a wanted man. At its coarsest polarity, the question was 'Did he fall, or was he pushed?' The permutations of the old tragedy are still hotly discussed. They go like this...

– The death was a pure accident: Rose fell and all the injuries were caused by that fall.

– Laurie pushed Rose down, and he died of the resultant injuries.

– Laurie pushed Rose down, and then finished him off with a stone.

– Laurie ascended Goatfell with the full, premeditated intention of killing Rose; i.e. he was a dangerous homicidal maniac, muttering, withdrawn and restless.

– Laurie, a known thief, ascended Goatfell with the full, premeditated intention of robbing Rose. Some violence to that end might have been in contemplation.

– In order to rob, and to escape, Laurie knew that only outright murder would succeed.

– At the summit, a sudden brainstorm overcame Laurie, a disturbed individual, and a town-rat, as a result of the dizzy surroundings, the exertion, and the toothache. Thus inflamed, he turned on Rose and felled him.

– It began as an accident. On the tricky descent, Rose slipped and hurt himself. Looking down at the fallen man in his finery, helpless, the De'il entered into Laurie's unstable mind, and he murdered for gain on sudden impulse.

– There was an argument or confrontation when they drew breath at the summit. Money could have been an issue. Sex, too. Suppose that Rose had made an approach to Laurie in the shared bed in which fate had placed them in such heady conditions of privacy. (Or vice versa.) Suppose that some covert sexual ambivalence lurked deep in Laurie, and confusing shame and recognition had overwhelmed him.

– If the death had been accidental, the concealment of the body was an act of panic, because Laurie feared that he would not be believed. The thefts from the body and its concealment were not necessarily a concomitant of murder.

And so the alternatives breed and multiply. Laurie gave them his full attention. As he escaped from the island, the intention, or effect, of the concealment of the body, whether an improvised endeavour, or pre-planned, was to allow 'John Annandale' to disappear, and John Laurie to revert unsuspected to his previous existence.

As a matter of fact, the concealment of the body may be a sign that murder was not premeditated. If the old photographs of the scene of the crime are studied, it can be seen that the ground is singularly bare of cover, treeless, with no hope of digging into the granite. Only rocks and boulders were available. Anything like a new cairn would have been conspicuous. There were other walkers around, and someone might have looked down from the ridge and seen what Laurie was about. The concealment was cunningly executed, and lasted for longer than he could have hoped.

Recklessly, he had not returned immediately to his life as John Laurie in Glasgow, but had retraced his steps to his previous lodgings at Port Bannatyne, Rothesay, where he was known as 'John Annandale', and coolly sat out the remains of the holiday which he had interrupted for his stay in Arran. He strutted around wearing Rose's chocolate-brown striped tennis jacket and yachting cap.

James Gillon Aitken was the man who forged the link between Laurie and 'Annandale', and Laurie should have feared him and avoided him at all costs. He was a grain merchant from 3 Lansdowne Place, Shawlands, Glasgow, and he knew Laurie under his real name from having met him in Rothesay the previous year. This year, he was actually on the *Ivanhoe* when Rose made the fatal connection with Laurie. He saw them together. And when, back at Rothesay, he met Laurie again, he could not help noticing that he was wearing a cap very similar to his new friend's. It was on the tip of his tongue to say so.

When they were both home in Glasgow, they met by chance in Hope Street, and Laurie tried to bluff it out. By that time (July 31st) the disappearance of Edwin Rose was in all the newspapers. 'What do you know about the Arran mystery?' Aitken asked, blunt and suspicious. Was not Rose the name of the tourist he had intended to go to Brodick with?

Laurie 'hummed and hawed'. The man a'missing, he lied like a schoolboy, 'Must be a different Mr Rose from the Mr Rose who was with me, for he returned with me and then proceeded to Leeds.'

Persisting, Aitken 'twitted' him about the yachting cap: 'Whose cap were you wearing on yon Friday night?' 'Surely you don't think I am a...' (He did not finish the sentence, but Aitken thought that the word hovering could have been 'thief' not 'murderer'). Laurie's luck had now evaporated and once the body had been found, he decamped and went on the run – always prone to flee, a great if ultimately unsuccessful escapee – increasingly losing his grip, rootless, but not over troubled with his conscience. Alerted by Aitken, the police followed his trail to Liverpool, where, at 10 Greek Street, he had abandoned some white shirts which had belonged to Rose and upon which, with a rubber stamp, he had impressed 'John W. Laurie'. From Liverpool, he had written on August 10th to the *North British Daily Mail* an egregious letter, not at all insane, in which he sought, rather childishly, to give the impression that he was about to commit suicide. Should that fail, he was also rehearsing his defence. Written in a fair, board school hand, in the style of a Marie Corelli romance, salient passages read: 'I rather smile when I read that my arrest is hourly expected. If things go as I have designed them, I will soon have arrived at that country from whose bourne no traveller returns...

As regards Mr Rose, poor fellow, no-one who knows me will believe for one moment that I had any complicity in his death... We went to the top of Goatfell, where I left him in the company of two men who came from Loch Ranza, and were going to Brodick.'

Some content of the letter can be taken as a proclamation of Laurie's heterosexuality. It can, too, if we wish, be taken to show anti-social conduct, morbid jealousy, with a paranoid flavour:

'Three years ago I became very much attached to Miss —, a teacher, — School, and residing at —. My affection for this girl was at first returned ... until I discovered that she was encouraging the attentions of another man, —, teacher, —, who took every opportunity to depreciate me in her estimation. Since then I have been perfectly careless about what I did, and my one thought was how to punish her enough for the cruel wrong she had done me; and it was to watch her audacious behaviour that I went to Rothesay this and last year.'

Was it thoughts of the perfidious teacher which tormented Laurie's mind as he paced the lane behind Wooley's Tea Rooms? Was she lucky, perhaps not to have been subjected to some murderous assault by his hands – pushed from the pier to drown without pity? We may feel that the superior social class of the teacher, and the usurper, together with that of Edwin Rose, was a part of the darkness in Laurie's mind.

A second letter, this time to the editor of the *Glasgow Herald*, dated August 27th and posted in Aberdeen, suggested that, 'Seemingly there was a motive for doing away with poor Rose; it was not to secure his valuables. Mr Rose was to all appearance worse off than myself; indeed, he assured me that he had spent so much on his tour that he had barely sufficient to last till he got home.'

Run to earth in a wood some three miles from Hamilton, he was found with his throat cut, but not too deeply. 'I robbed the man, but I did not murder him' he said in an important admission. He was from now on willing to own up to the items which he had stolen from Mrs Walker's 'lie-to', but it proved difficult to establish that he had taken items from Rose's pockets on the mountainside. Did he mean that Rose died by accident and he rifled the body there and then and hid it, or did he imply that others did the deed after he had left Rose intact?

The second alternative was certainly the force of his defence at the trial in Edinburgh which opened on November 8th, 1889. The Dean of Faculty argued for him that all of Rose's injuries were consistent with an accidental fall, and very likely, 'at these Fair holidays, there would be plenty of people on the island who would steal from the body.' The Prosecution adhered to the plain theory of repeated blows by Laurie with a stone, followed by theft at the scene. Weighty and learned medical experts brought for either side effectively cancelled one another out, as was reflected in the verdict of Guilty, by a majority of one, seven voting for Not Proven. Hangman Berry would soon be required. An agitation, however, gained strength, based on the feeling that Laurie must have been insane to have performed such a gross, excessive and inappropriate series of acts. A petition pleaded that there was insanity in Laurie's family and that he himself had a significant history. This had not been an issue at the trial, where the defence was a classic criminal's fight against circumstantial evidence. A visiting lunacy commission was convened, and the convicted man was pronounced insane.

He was very, very lucky. An available statistic for English crime shows that in 1893, of the 256 prisoners sentenced to death for murder in the previous nine years, only eight were committed to Broadmoor as insane, 145 were hanged, one was pardoned and 102 were sent to penal servitude.

Somewhere in official records the alientists' report must lie. It is difficult to conceive that Laurie was suffering from 'mania', as they called schizophrenia in those days. Perhaps they found his illness to be 'meloncholia': there may have been previous suicide attempts. His obsession about the teacher could have been accounted a 'monomania'. Or perhaps the diagnosis was 'moral insanity', an abandoned term closest to our 'psychopathy', defined by Dr JC Pritchard (1786-1848) as 'Madness consisting in a morbid perversion of the natural feelings, affections, inclinations, temper, habits, moral disposition and natural impulses without any remarkable disorder or defect in the intellect...'

The death sentence was commuted to penal servitude for life, and Laurie was held at Perth Penitentiary, and then Peterhead. He escaped in thick fog in 1893, but was quickly caught by a warder on a bicycle. In 1910, he was transferred to Perth Criminal Asylum, which was a department of Perth Penitentiary, not a separate asylum. He was by now suffering from progressive dementia, i.e. some type of deteriorating process, not insanity. There he died on October 5th 1930, aged 69. It was said that he had enquired about confessing before he was respited, but as Dr Forbes Winslow, the celebrated English alienist who was about at that time, and who would undoubtedly have found him insane, said in another context, 'Of course, it was only to be expected that after Mrs Pearcey's death [by judicial hanging, after murdering her lover's wife and baby] a full confession would be circulated far and wide. This is always done to justify carrying out the last operation of the law'.

CHAPTER 2
THE GERMAN
TEA-PLANTER

The victim in the Broughty Ferry case was universally described as an elderly, rich, eccentric recluse. This is a stereotype. The author is no fierce feminist, but has always thought that contemporary writers diminished Miss Jean Milne's posthumous dignity. Let us look at each element of the labelling in turn. Her age was 65, not ancient, and William Roughead, who should have known better and himself lived to a good old, productive age, would persist in calling her a 'little frail old woman'. This was no wispy, gossamer person, but sprightly, and she lived with hope.

Rich she certainly was, on her income of £1,000 per year in 1912. Her main expense, or extravagance, was to spend months at a time on holiday in London hotels. She also bought clothes and she gave unknown sums to charity. Her money came to her upon the death, nine years previously, of her brother, who was a tobacco manufacturer of Dundee. She had lived on, alone, in the substantial house which they had shared.

Now we come to the eremitical element. No woman who had really given up the world would regularly go away on sprees to the capital, staying at smartish hotels such as the Bonnington and the Strand Palace. No real hermit is seen every Sunday on show in church, attends Home Mission meetings, and tours the Highlands. Hermits do not have telephones. It is surprising, moreover, how many people came forward with gossip and called themselves friends of a woman supposedly so isolated.

Finally, and the last two elements merge, she was stamped

with the seal of eccentricity. If only we knew more of her private history, there could be a solid explanation of her circumstances. She might always have been a little different. Whatever the hereditary factors, past events, old frustrations or sadnesses, she was still interested, very interested, in the company of men.

Her choice of living without companion or servant was eccentric. This must be conceded. There were ample funds for a married couple to be engaged to keep her large Victorian property, Elmgrove House, and its two-acre garden in a decent state of equilibrium, although, as we now recognise, the most respectable-seeming butler can become seized with jealous rapacity. There is a certain type of religious woman who trusts that God will watch over her, and closes her mind to the evil in the world. Miss Milne may very well have been of this disposition. It is not fearlessness, but innocence.

Perhaps, too, she reasoned that the city was dangerous, and her decorous suburb was safe. She could hardly have been unaware of the fate of Miss Marion Gilchrist, aged 82, who had been murdered in her own home in Glasgow in 1908, in spite of impressive security apparata and a living-in servant. The truth is that both women were magnets to malefactors. A dog would have been a good idea. Miss Gilchrist's red Irish terrier would have made her killer think twice when the moment came, but he had been poisoned.

The most eccentric element of Miss Milne's life-style must be her neglect of the house. No doubt she calculated that it would see her out, and would survive, as indeed it did, even if most of the 14 rooms were never used nor touched. She had carved out for herself a capsule of one bedroom upstairs, one living-room downstairs, and a kitchen and bathroom. Did she sometimes wander those closed and cobwebbed rooms with candle in hand in the mode of Miss Faversham? One feels that she would have known her Dickens and her Scott, but her favourite reading was of the devotional kind. Candlelight flickered as she read with undrawn blinds late into the evening, for it was a personal quirk that she used gas only for cooking and heating. Did she look under the bed at night, and lock the bedroom door?

She worried more about the garden than the housework, employing jobbing gardeners from time to time, and she went out with rake and trowel herself, but it was an impossible task, and a wilderness had overtaken her. She kept remarkably cheerful, and this, then, was the setting for the murder of Miss Jean Milne, which is still unsolved, a mystery left to futurity in a state of muddlement. Who was the gentleman friend who came to supper? And who was the woman seen at the upper window when Miss Milne lay dead below?

During that last year of 1912, something 'kittenish' had been observed in her behaviour. She had spent four months at the Strand Palace from April 9th to August 2nd, and while there, as she indiscreetly told her occasional gardener, John Wood, she had met a 'German gentleman', a tea-planter. A woman friend found her positively coquettish when she confided that she had met a gentleman who had taken her about and been so very kind to her. It was not beyond the bounds of possibility, she hinted, that she was going to acquire a companion for life.

She expected a letter from him, and it appears that he travelled up to see her, because at 5.30pm on September 19th, John Wood who was 'shutting up the house' and about to leave, admitted a visitor bearing all the hallmarks of being the German tea-planter. 'You have come!' Miss Milne is said to have cried, skipping along the passage 'like a lassie' to greet him. 'I expected you earlier.' Imagine the gossip which will have burned around that genteel neighbourhood!

The following day, she left Broughty Ferry for Glasgow, where she embarked in the *Chevalier* for a cruise around the coast to Inverness. On the return journey, someone recognised her on board the Caledonian Canal steamer in the company of a tall, handsome man, with whom she left the boat at Fort Augustus. By September 26th, she was home again, resuming her normal routine.

John Wood later supplied a detailed description of the expected visitor. He was about 40 years old, some five feet eight or nine inches in height, stoutish and well-made, with fair hair and a slight fair moustache, fresh complexion, and a cheery expression. He was elaborately dressed in a dark morning-coat, deep cut waistcoat and dark trousers, and the whole topped somewhat incongruously with a soft, round tweed hat. He carried a cane to complete the gentlemanly effect. The voice that issued was deep and guttural. Who could reasonably doubt that this pyknic figure was the German tea-planter in person?

We may contemplate this apparition with some anxiety. What were his intentions? Miss Milne obviously felt that the kindly attentions which he had paid to her were romantic. It would be cruel to mock her. William Roughead refers to her misfortunately as 'in her new avatar [incarnation] of an antique charmer'. This might have been side-splitting at the time, but now seems like a disservice to the 'venerable anchorite of Broughty Ferry'.

Although, of course, such things do happen, the age-gap of 25 years would appear to be too extreme. Why would he have approached this singularly unprotected lady in the public rooms of a hotel? What could she have known reliably of his background? Suppose that all were platonic, even if she did not view it thus: a mere holiday friendship, a lonely foreigner, a genuine desire to help so vulnerable a creature and a shared liking of devotional literature? Yet he does not sound like a man who would lack company.

It is very difficult to dismiss the suspicion that the real interest of this urbane man of the world lay in Miss Milne's wealth. It is not necessary to suggest that he was an actual con-man – although he might have been. Down on his luck, perhaps, he might have spotted a glint of the seven valuable rings which she sported on her fingers when dressed up, or even when tending her garden. They were a token of her real status in life, however passée the figure that she cut, and he might have seen the light of hope. Miss Milne, meanwhile, was experiencing a different kind of hope.

Towards the middle of October, she ordered some wine and whisky from a local merchant, specifying that they should be of the same quality as her brother used to get. 'I am expecting a gentleman friend to dinner', she told him proudly. The sadness of this incident nearly speaks for itself. And then, the last time that she was seen alive was on Tuesday October 15th, scuttling about her business in Dundee and Broughty Ferry. The previous Sunday, she had attended St Andrew's United Free Church, and on Monday 14th she had been at a Home Mission meeting in Dundee. After her shopping expedition on that Tuesday, she was missed, her absences remarked, but not so acutely that anyone felt inspired to take action until the postman, for the usual obvious reasons, went to the police on Saturday November 2nd.

On Wednesday October 16th, after sunset, David Kinnear, an elder of the church had called at Elmgrove with her Communion card for the following Sunday, but found the house in darkness without the glow of candlelight. He knocked and rang repeatedly but there was no response and he went away. No Miss Milne came to church on the Sunday. On Friday October 18th, a telephone operator tried with admirable old-fashioned persistence to put a trunk call through to Elmgrove from London.

On Monday morning, October 21st, the mysterious woman at the window appeared. Alexander Troup saw her. He had been a gardener at Elmgrove in the days when Miss Milne's brother was alive, but appeared now (should one say in his avatar) as collector for the Broughty Benevolent Trust. When he came to tell his tale, he had not, apparently mistaken the day, because his statement was corroborated as to his being despatched then to Elmgrove. As he approached the house, he saw at an upper window, partly hidden by the curtain, a woman whom he identified as Miss Milne. Although he rang the front-door bell twice, there was no reply. The cover of the lock was down, and when he returned in the afternoon, it was up. Again, no-one opened the door, and the windows were blank. He went away.

Troup's sighting cannot be taken at its face-value, but still needs to be examined. As an officer entrusted with funds, it is not likely that he was a liar, an alcoholic, or otherwise of confused mental state. The woman's shape was not a clinical hallucination. It could have been a ghost – of Miss Milne, or of someone else. How good was Troup's eyesight? It could have been a trick of light, an honest mistake, the more so since he expected to see Miss Milne (perhaps she had often peered down at him when he called) or was looking especially closely for her, having heard that she had not recently been seen around. If he saw a real woman, it was not Miss Milne.

On Sunday morning, November 3rd 1912, when Miss Milne should have been preparing for church, the police approached the cold and silent house and forced an entry through the locked front door. Other exits and windows were long disused and 'hermetically sealed'. A joiner broke a window-pane in the kitchen, opened the catch, climbed in, and in some manner breached the front-door lock. He will have been the first person to see Miss Milne's body, which lay, fully dressed, in the hall, at the foot of the stairs.

This was no hermit's natural end. There had been a violent struggle. On the third step of the stairs there was a large splash of blood, and more on the railings and wall, with some blood-stained hairs adhering. Several wounds to the head were the apparent cause of death, and death's instrument lay in blood beside the body: the same poker which Miss Milne had often flourished as she chased away the apple-scrumping boys who trespassed into her wilderness. Therefore, this was the weapon which she would have taken up if the occasion should have arisen – if she had time and opportunity. The force of the attack had actually broken the poker. It was about 13 inches long, made of ordinary cast-metal, with a round head. The break was new because it had broken about half an inch from the head, and both parts bore stains of blood.

Imbued with some vestige of super-ego, unless the intention was concealment, the assailant had partly covered the body with a sheet. The glass door in the hall had been blocked out by tying the curtains in a certain way with a length of common (gardening?) twine. All the murderer's tools were improvisations, not imported as by malice, but borrowed from the immediate domestic environment. Miss Milne was surely still alive when her ankles were tightly bound together with a curtain-cord. The telephone wire had been cut. Professional criminals did that, but not generally with a pair of garden shears. These lay, still *in situ*, in the hall accompanied by a rake and a hoe. She had not necessarily been gardening. With Miss Milne all things were possible, and she might have kept her tools in the hall as a matter of course. The improviser had not stooped to wrench from the fingers of the dead or dying woman those seven precious rings which now ornamented the hands of a corpse. Her gold watch and chain lay openly on the toilet-table in the bedroom, and her silver was untouched. The sum of £17 in gold was found in a purse or handbag in a drawer. She had drawn £20 in gold from her bank at the end of September, and this was assumed to be the balance.

The *Mary Celeste* scene in the living or dining-room was a clue in itself. The table was laid for high tea for two people, with a two-penny meat pie as its centre-piece. This must have been at that time a handsome pork-pie, and not so miserly as it sounds, especially since Miss Milne had not stinted on the liquid refreshments. All fingerprints were soon lost, as the police flailed about in their unsophisticated search.

A post-mortem was very soon carried out. It disclosed that the body was marked all over with many blows inflicted by a heavy instrument such as the poker. Death was caused by cerebral haemorrhage due to blows to the head which, although numerous, were relatively slight. no-one injury would have killed: it was the totality, and the shock, which ended the life of Miss Jean Milne. Undigested food found in the stomach indicated that she had not long survived the attack.

The hall at Elmgrove in November must have been cold, with the body lying very possibly on tiles, and therefore better preserved than in a warmer environment. Any miscalculation by those performing the post-mortem would have, notionally, put the real date of death further back in time, and would not favour Troup's sighting, which was too recent.

On Monday November 4th, Detective Lieutenant Trench, of the Glasgow City Police was called in for his known expertise in difficult cases. The resemblance to the case of Miss Gilchrist, in which he was later to play an important part, was not lost on him. The Chief Constable of Broughty Ferry, Howard Sempill, escorted him to Elmgrove, where he made some new findings. The local force could hardly have missed the bloodstained towel lying near the kitchen sink, positively saturated with DNA – perhaps some from the killer – if these things had been known, but Trench also found the imprint of three fingers on a piece of paper in the same area. Sent off to New Scotland Yard, (where the Fingerprint Branch had been set up in 1901) they proved to be too blurred to be of any use.

A half-smoked cigar butt – more DNA! – was found by Trench in the ashes of the grate in the dining-room. This was thought to be a very significant clue, but in fact, it is an ambiguous object. We are told that Miss Milne used gas for heating, but we cannot know for sure if gas was laid to a heater in the dining-room, so that we do not know how often she lit a coal fire in that room. Neighbours did notice that no smoke came from the chimneys of Elmgrove during the 'missing period'. Common sense tells us that she lit a fire when she expected company. We can have no confidence in her assiduity in regularly cleaning out the grate. The ashes could have been the remains of a fire which pre-dated the murder. We know that the German tea-planter was present in the room on September 19th, and the cigar could have fallen from him on that occasion. The point is that the cigar did not necessarily come from the lips of the murderer, nor from the gentleman caller expected to supper (keeping the two personages separate for the time being). It could even have come to rest in the cold ashes after the murder. A member of the investigating and cleaning-up party could have been the culprit.

The cigar was also thought to clinch the gender of the murderer (unless an invader from *The Well of Loneliness*). Troup's woman at the window, and the comparative lightness of the killing blows, had been imagined to betray a female hand, but this was merely fanciful. Probably the inadequacy of the weapons available was relevant in this context; the poker was not a large one, and, indeed, it broke.

All in all, however, it is a reasonable view that the cigar came with the murderer. The fact that it was only half-smoked may be a clue. Although it is usual to light up *after* a meal, the timing is not written in stone. Addiction, as it were, could outweigh polite custom. A foreigner might have different habits. Could anyone draw on a cigar after committing murder? Miss Milne does not appear to have sat down with her visitor to demolish the pie. Information as to the state of the bottles of wine and whisky is sadly lacking. The inference is that (unless he was trying to give them up!) the pre-prandial smoker threw away the cigar half-consumed because he was distracted or interrupted. The meal was announced. Something happened. There was a change of plan. Or all hell let loose.

The significance of the carving fork had been missed by previous investigators. It had been found in the hall, half-hidden beneath a chest. A sharpish, two-pronged implement, it belonged to the carving set from the sideboard in the dining-room. It could actually have been laid on the table ready for use on that notable pork pie. Trench examined Miss Milne's last clothes, and discerned in the blouse and under-garments a number of double punctures which matched the fork. He applied without success for the exhumation of the body, which had been swiftly buried on November 5th in the Western Cemetery, Dundee. It seems incalculable that the post-mortem report had made no mention of puncture wounds. Either they had been missed, or the fork had not penetrated the layers of clothing.

William Roughead was content to stay with the official theory that there had been no theft from Elmgrove, but it appears that he was not familiar with Detective Trench's feature on the case which appeared in the *Weekly News* on May 1st 1915. Here Trench stated that in addition to the handbag containing £17 in gold, he had also found three more handbags which were devoid of money – two small ones on the dining-room table and another one in the bedroom. 'It is remarkable', the article reads, 'that a lady who was travelling on the [tram] cars and who made small purchases on the last occasion she was seen alive should not have had some silver or gold about her... I believe that the person who committed the crime probably got a considerable sum of money from Miss Milne's handbag.' Well, maybe, but there could be simple reasons why she had no loose change about her.

Was Trench, then, adverting to, in Roughead's words, 'the theory of the casual tramp or peripatetic burglar, so dear to the official mind'? Indeed he was: 'In my own mind I have reconstructed the crime, and have come to the conclusion that the murderer had slipped into the house by the front-door while Miss Milne was in the grounds collecting flowers and pieces of holly to decorate the dining-room table, and also gathering some apples, for a number of apples which had been taken from the orchard were found in the house.' Trench remarked, incidentally, that the large dining-room table was littered with books and papers of every description (with a dell hewed out for the feast, presumably, unless, it is to be hoped, that was set out on a side-table). It is not recorded that dried-up holly and flowers were found in disarray in the hall or dining-room.

However, Trench does not address the problem of the missing gentleman caller. Common sense tells us that he was the German tea-planter. He had already been a welcome visitor. Miss Milne would not have harboured high hopes of more than one man. It is very, very suspicious that he vanished from the face of the earth. Any decent man of good character, knowing that Miss Milne lived alone, and finding her house locked, silent and dark, when he arrived for a meal by pre-arrangement, would have run for help. His first, or even second, thought would not have been for his own situation.

A reward of £100 was put up. Margaret Campbell, a maid at the house next door, which had a good view of Miss Milne's wilderness, came forward to say that one morning in the second week of October, at about 10.30, she was surprised to see a gentleman in those previously virgin grounds. He paced up and down a garden-path, slowly, with bent head and his hands in his pockets. His hair seemed to be fair and his features round, and we may in all reason take this to be the German tea-planter waiting to call upon Miss Milne at a respectable hour. It matters not at all that the maid estimated his height to be six feet. The fact that she thought he was wearing evening-dress (as if he had come straight from the flesh-pots of Dundee and had not seen his bed that night) is stranger to explain, but it may well be that the maid had mistaken his elaborate calling uniform of continental cut!

We may confidently discount, as did the police, the sinister passenger from the South train at Dundee who hailed a taxi at 1am on the calculated day of the murder, Tuesday October 15th, and ordered the driver, Frederick Ewing, to drive him to Broughty Ferry. He had a fierce demeanour, and a piercing eye, and, like Jack the Ripper in person, he carried a small handbag. He asked to be dropped 'in the vicinity of Elmgrove'. He was of the requisite good build and height – about five feet nine inches – and Aryan colouring with a pale complexion and 'slight fair moustache'. Unfortunately, he spoke with an English accent. The dustman's sighting is a different matter entirely. At 4.30am on the morning after the murder, Wednesday October 16th, the day when Elder Kinnaird called after sunset, James Don was working his way along Grove Road. The morning was not a dark one, and there was a gas-lamp near the entrance to Elmgrove. At the gate, the dustman saw a stranger trying to leave the property without being seen (although one would have thought that he would have heard the noise that Don must have been making). The furtive man drew back, but realising that he had been spotted, decided to bluff it out, and left at a smart pace. From a distance of ten yards, the dustman noted that he was between 30 and 40 years of age, five feet eight or nine inches in height, weighing 11 to 12 stones, with sharp (not cheery) features, a very pale complexion, and slight fair moustache. He did not speak. He wore a bowler hat and dark overcoat, with the collar turned up, and he looked like a gentleman.

It is very tempting to identify this ghastly-pale figure (if everything was as it was said to be) as the German, a murderer, who had lingered overnight in the house, pondering his options, and sneaked out when he, wrongly, calculated that the coast was clear. The other possibility which springs to the mind is that the wilderness at Elmgrove was used for clandestine purposes such as homosexual activity.

The murder was not premeditated. Perhaps the German tea-planter said or did something that betrayed his ultimate venal intentions. Miss Milne suddenly became frightened, and, realising her compromising situation, sought to escape, to run up the stairs to lock herself into her bedroom. Perhaps, in a panic, she attacked him first and there was some terrible preliminary duel, she armed with the poker, he with the carving fork. The reason why, unmasked, he should have resorted to extreme violence, lies in unknown regions of his mind. When he realised that he had gone too far, although she was not dead, he disabled her by tying her up, and cut the telephone wire so that

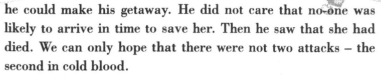

he could make his getaway. He did not care that no-one was likely to arrive in time to save her. Then he saw that she had died. We can only hope that there were not two attacks – the second in cold blood.

The fire went out of the investigation after Trench managed to avert a miscarriage of justice. Quite a number of witnesses, in the grip of some form of mass hysteria, confidently identified a Canadian rolling-stone, named Charles Warner, as the suspicious character seen in the vicinity of Elmgrove. In a practice now beyond the pale, they were shown photographs of Warner before picking him out on identification parade. The poor fellow was a sitting target, held at Maidstone prison for fraudulently obtaining bed and board at the Rose and Crown, at Tonbridge. Trench went to Antwerp to confirm his alibi, which he had almost forgotten, his waistcoat pawned at the time of the murder.

If he survived World War 1, the German tea-planter may be imagined, not very robust, exiled on some rickety verandah in a jungly colony not even German any longer. Grey now, grim not cheery, reaching for his bottle of quinine and wedded to his cigars, he would try very hard not to remember the nightmare in Scotland.

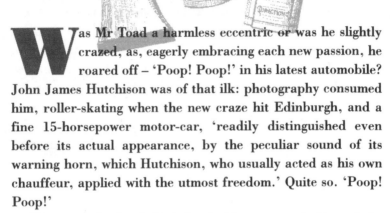

CHAPTER 3
THE LATE MR TOAD

Was Mr Toad a harmless eccentric or was he slightly crazed, as, eagerly embracing each new passion, he roared off – 'Poop! Poop!' in his latest automobile? John James Hutchison was of that ilk: photography consumed him, roller-skating when the new craze hit Edinburgh, and a fine 15-horsepower motor-car, 'readily distinguished even before its actual appearance, by the peculiar sound of its warning horn, which Hutchison, who usually acted as his own chauffeur, applied with the utmost freedom.' Quite so. 'Poop! Poop!'

His general mien belied the dashing outward show of the vehicle. We have an unusually precise description, down to the state of his dentition: 'John James Hutchison, a chemist, about 24 years of age, but looks older, about six feet in height, medium build, brown hair, clean shaven, sharp features, fresh complexion, false teeth (both sets), gentlemanly appearance, and of good address, stoops forward when walking, native of Dalkeith. Dressed when last seen in dark brown tweed suit, heavy brown motor coat, light green felt hat, white stand-up collar, with turned-down peaks, and tie. Was wearing gold watch and chain and two gold signet rings, one of which is set with diamonds on clasped hands.'

Recently, in 1911, Hutchison had shown signs of going off the rails. He had abandoned his perfectly decent job as chemist at his uncle's firm in Musselburgh and taken to speculation on the Stock Exchange. During the rubber boom, he claimed, he had made the sum of £17,000. Other investments, however, in copper, oils, and South African shares had proved inadvisable, although he had recommended them to friends as a good thing. He had taken to tearing around the streets of Dalkeith, where, at Bridgend, he lived with his parents, as if the speed of his car relieved the anxiety of his financial status. There was talk about him.

The fact that he was engaged to be married appears to have given him no comfort. His fiancée was extraneous to his real problems. Meanwhile, with what might have appeared to him to be callous indifference to their only son's debts – his precious motor-car had been seized in part satisfaction of an account due to a firm of Edinburgh stockbrokers and was standing forlornly in a Dalkeith garage – his parents were stolidly making preparations for their silver wedding party. Charles Hutchison, paterfamilias, was a solid man of good report, a Freemason, and employed on the estates of the Duke of Buccleuch, at Dalkeith. The refreshments were to be of the finest, and the coffee was purchased specially, on the day of the party, in order to be fresh, from a Musselburgh grocer named Clapperton.

That evening, Friday February 3rd, 1911, after supper, John Hutchison, lanky, stooping son of the house, politely handed round coffee to the well-fed, grateful guests. Three abstained, but fifteen drank deep. All too soon, the scene disintegrated into a groaning battlefield, with vomiting, purging figures in panic and disarray. Some ran out into the freezing garden, and lay where they fell. Others writhed on sofas and on the floors of the bespattered house. Of those who administered relief to the sufferers, none was more attentive with bowl and cloth than John Hutchison, himself unaffected by the sudden malady. His fiancee was among those stricken. Two local doctors were summoned to the disaster and they called in a consultant physician from Edinburgh, but they failed to save Charles Hutchison, who, hearty on his celebration day, had quaffed down a full cup of coffee, nor Clapperton, the grocer, appreciative of his own product. Both died within a few hours.

In due course, everyone else recovered, although Mrs Hutchison's case was touch-and-go.

Professor Harvey Littlejohn, who held the chair of Medical Jurisprudence at Edinburgh University, conducted the double post-mortem on Sunday February 5th, with the doctors who had tried to save the two victims in attendance. He found no natural cause of death, and his suspicion of arsenical poisoning was soon confirmed by chemical analysis of certain portions of the intestines. Freemasonry was very well represented at Mr Hutchison's funeral. The chief mourner at Eskbank Cemetery was John Hutchison, and none saw anything save grief in his demeanour. Many of those present, including the last-named, moved on that same afternoon to attend the Clapperton funeral at Musselburgh. There was an assemblage of some five hundred, among whom, no doubt, were a few shaken silver wedding guests.

On February 10th, it was officially announced that arsenic had been found in the remains of the party coffee. It was not present in Mr Clapperton's stock in his shop, to which no suspicion was attached, nor in the portion of ground coffee left unused at the house. It was not present in either the milk or the sugar served with the coffee. In other words, arsenic was found in the coffee pot or pots, or in the discarded cups which had still contained coffee, or in both. Therefore, a hand must have doctored the pots, or slipped arsenic into each and every cup somewhere on its way from pot to recipient, which would seem to be a tricky manoeuvre to perform 15 times.

Shock and bewilderment informed Dalkeith. Some inexplicable accident was the subject of discussion. John Hutchison was not at first a suspect, although it was no secret that he had been the bearer of the poisoned coffee. He must have proffered an excuse for his own immunity. His person was not searched until it was too late. His concern for the victims was very convincing. The realisation that he had dispensed drugs from his uncle's shop did, however, eventually concentrate the minds of the police investigators. Going over to Musselburgh, they found that a bottle of arsenic had disappeared from the shelves, with no record of sale in the poisons register.

Meanwhile, on February 14th, John Hutchison had left home to visit, he said, some friends in Newcastle, pleading the equivalent of our new-fangled post-traumatic stress syndrome. He was expected back on February 16th, but failed to return, whereupon it was announced that a warrant had been issued for his arrest. On Saturday the 18th, a notice was broadcast to all police offices:

Wanted, on Sheriff's warrant, charged with murder by poisoning, John James Hutchison...

The notice stated that he had with him £25, mostly in gold, and carried a new brown leather handbag. He might now be wearing a dark brown coat. It was thought that he might be making for London and was probably intending to go abroad. All shipping offices and hotels were to be alerted. The detailed description of the wanted man was effective, because he was seen and recognised in the Strand, and Detective Inspector Laing went to London to work with Scotland Yard. All the local hotels were trawled, and he was found to have spent the night of Wednesday the 15th, at a hotel in Craven Street, which runs down beside Charing Cross station. He had acquired two aliases, John Robertson or Paterson, and a new Wanted notice was circulated by Scotland Yard.

Hutchison had had time to take ship for anywhere in the world, but, rudderless, he had dithered, and then been too clever for his own good. To a native of Dalkeith, no doubt, the Channel Islands seemed safe and remote, a fine and private place to hide away, but he had not calculated that Guernsey was just too tiny for a stranger not to be noticed, and the Wanted notice was just too particular.

On the boat from Southampton to Jersey, after huddling in a corner on the boat train, pretending to be asleep, with the collar of his heavy brown motor coat turned up, this fleeing man, who should have stayed a loner, became friendly with a fellow traveller and bombarded him with bogus information about himself. 'It looks like being a dirty passage,' was the remark with which he initiated their intercourse. JR Henderson was his latest name. He could not disguise his strong Scottish accent, but, he said, 'It is a very funny thing that although I am Scottish bred I have never been to Scotland.' His new friend seems to have been quite gullible.

From the depths of his subconscious, or even his unconscious, he drew the name of his principal dwelling in Ilford, where, he said, he owned three houses. This plangent name was Meldrondene, somehow redolent of rhododendrons, Melrose, melons and honey, and the author invites readers to provide a key. It sounds like some haven of his childhood, some sandy seaside home. He had no future, his present was too horrible to contemplate, and only the past of his childhood was bearable to visit, and so, now, he gibbered and fantasised: his father was a very wealthy man, fond of old furniture, he himself was a medical man, living on his means, and the doctors had ordered him to the Channel Islands for his health.

Over a drink in the smoke-room on the boat he expatiated on motor-cars and said that he had made £20,000 out of rubber, on an investment of £350. His companion noticed that he was growing a beard. They went ashore at Jersey together, and booked in at the Star Hotel, St Heliers. It was 10.30am and Hutchison was not seen again until dinner. He was in good spirits and said that he had slept all day. He was going to get married in July. After dinner, the conversation turned to recent crimes. 'What do you think of the Houndsditch and Clapham murders?' he asked. 'It is strange that they can't catch Peter the Painter.' London was the best place in the world for a criminal to hide away.

The next morning, they left by boat for Guernsey, Hutchison buying a single ticket. The friend made for the Queen's Hotel, but he chose a boarding-house. 'To tell you the truth,' he said, 'I am a little bit hard up, and had to find a cheaper place, otherwise I should have stayed with you. I usually take only a certain amount with me, as I am afraid of being robbed.' The friend swallowed all this. In the evening they walked about the little town of St Peter Port, and, Mr Toad asserting himself, they visited a skating-rink.

'I am sorry I can't ask you to have a drink with me,' Hutchison confessed, 'but when I come to London I hope to entertain you to dinner. I am afraid I shall have to pawn my rings as it is!' The good friend offered to lend him a sovereign. He accepted, saying he would give him a cheque for it.

After only a day , the good new friend who had given him some sense of reality, returned to London via Weymouth, and they said good-bye on the pier. He himself, he announced, was going to Monte Carlo. The last time he had been there, he had made enough money to pay all his expenses. He promised to write, from 'Meldrondene'. Suddenly, as if he could not wait, he bought two London newspapers from a seller on the pier. The friend made to look at the pictures, but he brushed him aside and scanned the pages, seeming very agitated. Apologising for his haste, he departed. Always a gentleman, he waved from the end of the quay.

On the train to London, the friend read the *Evening Times*, in which there was a description of the wanted man. Light dawned, he went straight to the police, and was shown a photograph of Hutchison. Very soon, on Monday, February 20th, Sergeant Burley of the Yard, equipped with a warrant, was knocking at the door of the boarding-house on the sea-front at St Peter Port. The sparkling beauty of the scene will have been lost to him: he knew that he was close to a desperate man, whom he probably regarded as a dangerous lunatic.

George Wright, the proprietor, let him in. PC Roberts was

stationed outside, in case of an attempted escape. Inside, all was deceptively calm. By coincidence, George Wright was reading a London newspaper which contained a picture of his lodger, and he was becoming uneasy. He showed the policeman the front parlour, which, with a bedroom, the lodger had taken on the preceding Friday. Burley opened the door and went in. All was calm. It was a tableau quivering on the edge of tragedy.

'I saw a young man sitting in an armchair,' he later deposed. 'His back was towards the door. He had a book in his left hand, and his right hand was in his trouser-pocket. I walked up close alongside him. I asked him his name. He said; "My name is Henderson". I said, "I have cause to believe your name is Hutchison". He replied, "You are making a great mistake, and I will prove that I am Henderson". I said, "Well, you come with me, please".'

The young man stood up, still keeping his right hand in his pocket. Naturally, the policeman must have feared a weapon of some kind. When they got near to the door, Hutchison made a rush up the stairs, taking two steps at a time. Burley followed right at his heels. There were ten steps in the first flight, and four in the second. The door of his bedroom was open. Just as he entered, he drew his hand from his pocket and raised it to his mouth. Burley saw not a weapon, but a phial of liquid. He struck out and sent the bottle flying across the room. The two men struggled, but only for an instant. The young man failed suddenly, and was laid out insensible on the floor.

Constable Roberts ran for a doctor, and within six minutes from ingestion of the liquid, Dr Bindloss was in the room and applying a stomach-pump. There was a strong smell of prussic acid from the phial, and no time was to be lost – stomach lavage was the appropriate specific treatment at the scene. Four minutes after his arrival, apparently, the dying man stopped breathing. Ten minutes dying was more merciful than the 'several hours' suffered by his father and the friendly grocer. The action of prussic acid, cyanide, is very rapid, as is well known. He will have hoped for instantaneous death, but he seems to have been unconscious anyway. The minimum fatal dose is about one grain (solid) and about 50 minims (liquid). It was said that the phial dashed away by Sergeant Burley would, if full, have contained enough to kill 16 people. A few drops were still left in it. We may well suspect that a bottle of prussic acid was missing from his uncle's shop in Musselburgh.

It was a classic chemist's suicide. For weeks, at least, he had had poison on his mind. Since he must have taken the cyanide with him to Guernsey, suicide was a pondered option if he were caught. Since he did not hold a return ticket, it might be argued that it was always his intention if he could form the resolution, and stop skating. More likely, he planned to lie low and then move on; he was obviously worried that his funds might not last. In reality, it is pretty clear that he had no idea what to do or where to go.

An unusual procedural situation had been caused by the death in Guernsey, and the inquest was held, on February 22nd, in the Police Court at St Peter Port, conducted by the Procureur du Roi. Five witnesses were called. Constable Roberts attested that when he had removed the body to the mortuary, he found a purse in one of the pockets which contained 15 sovereigns, three half-sovereigns, 18s. 6d. in silver, and 1s. 4d. in coppers. This was enough for a short siege. The jury returned a verdict of suicide from prussic acid poisoning. Detective Inspector Laing, of Edinburgh, who had known the deceased for six years, had identified the dead man as Hutchison, not Henderson, and arrangements were made for burial under the real name at the local cemetery. There was no call for a return of the body to Dalkeith, and there were said to be no mourners at the graveside. The mother was in no fit state to attend, even if she had wanted to do so. We cannot presume to know what her wishes were.

Hutchison had committed a very serious crime, a hair's-breadth from a mass murder of 15 (could have been 18) people.

The motive was obscure. It looked like an insane act, but his cool demeanour bothered those who sought for a merciful explanation. It was said that his father's life was insured for £4,000, but the details have not survived. The wholesale nature of the poisoning might have been intended to disguise the specificity of the intended effect – death of Father. Everyone knows that wedding guests are sometimes stricken with food poisoning. It is just possible that he found a way to administer a larger, killing dose to his father. The grocer who died, and his mother, who very nearly died, might both have had little resistance to the smaller dose, for some reason relating to their health. Or, alternatively, three doses prepared and calculated to kill might have been administered. The information which has come down to us that the father and the grocer drank deeper may have been a mere rationalisation.

Even so, it is tempting to hazard that there were psycho-pathological reasons, not just financial stress, for feeding poison to a multitude, for laying low the small, satisfied world of Bridgend – family, intended family, Freemasons and burghers – which oppressed a troubled mind. Soon, someone else would drive away his fine motor-car, his lost love-object.

'Poop! Poop!'

CHAPTER 4
'OH! LOCH MAREE!'

The composition of meals which figure in past murder trials has an interest all of its own. One thinks of the Bordens' breakfast at Fall River during a heat wave: warmed-up mutton broth, bread, bananas, johnnycake and coffee. Supper at 2 Wester Coates Terrace, Edinburgh, was a moveable feast before bedtime for the King family: bread and butter, cheese, jelly and coffee. An indigestible repast, one would have thought, and not even necessary, since steak or fish had already been consumed at tea-time.

The family of four that sat around the table in the parlour at about 9 o'clock on Friday evening, May 30th, 1924, presented a scene of unity: James Rae King, a chartered accountant, his wife, Agnes Scott King, and their two sons, William Laurie King, aged 22, and Alexis King, aged 16. The daily maid, Marion Armstrong, had gone home to 28 Wardlaw Place.

Behind the faÁade, however, there had been a brew of discontent which had simmered for years. It was to do with the frustration of a lad's true bent. Father wanted son to follow in his footsteps, but, since he was 12, William had yearned for a career in chemistry, for which he showed a natural aptitude. Indeed, a chemist friend, David Peebles, said that the boy knew more about chemistry than he did.

Tonight, there was in progress a resolution and conciliation. At last, Father had surrendered, a bitterly disappointed man. William was to read for a degree in chemistry at Edinburgh University. It was not too late for a change of direction. After attending Daniel Stewart's College, he had served two years of his apprenticeship with an outside firm of chartered accountants, but had been so unhappy there that his father had transferred his indenture to his own firm. As a sop, and a handsome one, James King had had an outhouse built for him in the back garden where he could tinker with his experiments to his heart's content. Still he had pined, and, worse, had hesitated to tell Father that he had not even attempted his Intermediate Chartered Accountancy examination. Mother had found out.

There are clues to indicate that Mother had not been very understanding. It had been a strict upbringing and she would not accept that William was an adult. It did not matter whether he resented her actions or not, she simply would not stop checking through his pockets. Her attitude towards the great passion in his life is evident in the telling words which she used when she found a packet of chemical substance in his pocket. 'What trash is this you have been buying, Willie?' she asked delicately. For some reason, too, the boys shared a bedroom, in a house which was quite spacious enough for privacy.

His father said that he knew nothing about it, but the fact is that William had been seeing a girl named Edith Ross, cashier at a garage, Liddle and Johnston's, Belford Road, where he had been sent to audit the firm's books, and where Father kept his car. William had given her a ring and a wristlet watch. She denied that they were engaged. Mother might have got wind of these secret matters, even if she did not tell her husband, because she had said to Marion Armstrong, the maid, that she was going to 'put William abroad'.

As things stood on May 30th, all should now have been well. William had just left Father's hated office, and the whole of the rest of his life glittered in chemical letters and formulae. He could afford to be grateful, generous and forgiving, because he had won. Unfortunately, he would have to be dependent on his family financially for some years yet. Father had been paying him a salary of £2.10s a month, and Mother gave him some pocket-money. An independent existence would come to him later than to others because of the false start which had been imposed on him. There had recently been a spot of trouble, when he had bought two cameras and had not been able to pay the account. Father had refused to help out, because he wanted to teach the lad that such things cost money.

Alexis, still a schoolboy, had just come in from tennis that Friday evening, and he was hungry again. Mother had set out the meal and made the coffee. Alexis put sugar in all four cups – it was a co-operative enterprise – and Mother poured in the coffee. William, as his duty, cut four slices of bread and handed one each to his parents balanced on the knife. Alexis grabbed the first slice which William had cut for him on the platter. Although he was the only one who did not take any cheese, it was Alexis who cut it for his parents. William took or got a smaller piece.

Father put his cheese on his bread and began to eat. He felt a burning sensation in his throat, and remarked that it was a funny bit of cheese that his wife had got that week. Piqued, perhaps, by the matrimonial slight, Mother had a second helping of the maligned cheese, together with the second half of Father's slice of bread; his appetite appeared to have diminished. Supper was over, and Mr King sat smoking by the fire. His wife and William sat beside him. Alexis tuned in on his wireless set. It was indeed a scene of domestic unity.

After a quarter of an hour, Mr King realised that he felt sick. He went up to bed, closely followed by Mrs King. Both vomited, and again, and again. There was bad pain in the stomach. Alexis was all right. William was sick three times (he said): downstairs, upstairs in the bathroom, and outside in the street. Alexis heard him vomiting downstairs in the pantry (where there was a sink).

Mr King asked for the doctor to be called. William reported that he had telephoned, but had been told that the doctor was out on a case, and it was not known when he would be back. Dr William Fraser Macdonald, of 42 Polwarth Terrace, later stated that he had been out on a confinement and when he arrived home at nearly midnight, there was no message for him on the slate, and he went to bed. This was taken to indicate that William had lied, but he was certainly right about the doctor's movements. He should have left a message.

In the absence of medical comfort, Mr King thought of the old stand-by, warming brandy, but had none in the house. William rang up the previously mentioned chemist, David Peebles, of 20 West Maitland Street to ask for a bottle, and left the house to fetch it. This was when he was sick for the third time, but unfortunately the chemist, who met him half-way, was not asked if he had noticed a pool of vomit in the gutter, or other signs. A dose of brandy sent Mr King to sleep, in the spare bedroom to which he had moved. At 12.30am he woke to vomit again. He looked into the main bedroom and asked the boys how their mother was. They said that she seemed to be much better (after the brandy) and he went back to bed.

Although Mr King did not seem to be aware of a second telephone call to the doctor (if there actually had been a first one) in fact, shortly after he had gone to bed, Dr Macdonald was telephoned by William and told about his parents' illness. He gathered that his attendance was not urgently required, and told William to let him know if the situation worsened. William's position at this stage is defensible. While they were in the bedroom with their mother, she cried out, 'Oh, Loch Maree, Loch Maree!' These strange, in fact sinking, words were a reference to a recent occasion when several guests at a Highland hotel had died from botulism after eating sandwiches filled with wild duck paste or pâté. The general apprehension, of course, in the stricken household was that the cheese had caused food-poisoning. Even stranger, Mother complained of seeing 'lights' in William's eyes, but not in Alexis's eyes. They switched off the electric light, thinking that she was bothered by reflection, but she still saw the lights in William's eyes in the darkness. This is a really uncomfortable image.

The boys went to bed. Alexis slept, and William said that he did, too. At 2am, Mr King woke up and was sick again. He staggered in to see his wife, and found that she was dead. She had slipped away, all on her own. He called the boys and told them to telephone his brother, Dr Robert King and David Peebles. Then he lay down in the library, where he spent the remainder of the night. He recovered. At 2.15am on his own initiative, William rang for Dr Macdonald.

The chill, dim house was suddenly ablaze with lights and thronged with people anxious to help and full of questions. Mr King lay on his sofa, helpless and bereaved. William, in great distress on his knees beside his dead mother, was heard to lament, in curiously stilted terms, 'Why was Mother taken and I not taken? Why did I not take my exam?' Mrs Peebles, wife of the chemist, arrived at 3.20am, saw the remains of a meal on the table, but did not notice any bread. (The loaf had not been intact, having been broached at tea-time, and the four slices taken at supper could have finished it, except, perhaps, for the end-crust.) She took all the cups, saucers and plates to the kitchen and washed them.

The doctors' joint and several opinion was that the cheese had been contaminated by an irritant poison, probably arsenic. On the morning of the following day, Detective Inspector David Fleming made the first of a number of visits to the house. He removed a glass jar of jelly, a tin box of coffee, and a paper bag of sugar, all found in the sideboard in the parlour. No cheese appeared to be left, so he visited the grocer's shop in Roseburn Terrace and appropriated the whole cheese from which the Kings' portion had been cut. On the Sunday, he took from the pocket of a grey jacket belonging to William, which was hanging in the wardrobe, a glass bottle containing a white powder and labelled Potass. Ferricyanide. He bore it away for analysis, together with other bottles from William's miniature laboratory in the back garden, where there was a great deal of photographic apparata. Two days later he was back at the house, asking about poisons – weed-killer, fly-killer, mouse-killer, rat-killer – but father and sons all stated categorically that they had no poisons whatsoever. The cheese, they said, must have been lethal. William was to say that he had never smelt or tasted a cheese like it, with a very sharp 'kick': the cheese-dish stank of it for three days after being washed (possibly by poor, kind Mrs Peebles!).

The post-mortem on the body of Mrs Agnes Scott King made by Professor Harvey Littlejohn on June 2nd had indicated that death had been caused by an irritant poison. She had been an apparently healthy woman, although it was known that she had been complaining of pain in the region of the heart, and had consulted Dr Macdonald. Any thoughts that she, rather than her husband, had succumbed because of some innate fragility were soon dispelled by the results of chemical analysis of internal organs. The horrifically large quantity of 3.01 grains of arsenious oxide (white arsenic in powder form) was found in the tissues tested, and, allowing for vomiting and purging, the computation was that the whole dose of arsenic taken in must have been in the region of 10 grains. The fatal dose in an adult is usually stated as from two to three grains. Mother had had no chance at all.

One week after the death, Detective Inspector Fleming was told at Surgeons' Hall that the glass bottle taken from the pocket of William's grey jacket actually contained three-quarters of an ounce of arsenious oxide, not potassium ferricyanide (which is comparatively less toxic, although capable of poisoning). Considerably activated by this discovery, he proceeded to the garage, Liddle and Johnston's, and triumphantly abstracted from the office two books which William had kept there: *Death and its Mystery at the Moment of Death*, and *Death and its Mystery after Death*. Rather more evidential than this adolescent reading matter, which Edith Ross knew all about, was the order form for '1lb arsenious oxide', in William King's handwriting, signed 'Liddle and Johnston', which a firm of wholesale chemical dealers, Baird's, of 39 Lothian Street, produced upon enquiry as to whether they had recently sold any arsenic. The clue which led Fleming to the dealers was a bottle found at the garage which bore the firm's label. On Tuesday June 10th, William was arrested in Douglas Gardens. After caution, he was searched, and some arsenic powder was found loosely adhering to the lining of the left hip-pocket of his trousers.

His splendid subsequent explanation deserves to be in a textbook of defences. Around May 26th, he said, he had his mind set on certain chemical experiments. He particularly wanted to derive a magenta dye from coal-tar, and he saw in his textbooks, (not, apparently, produced) that he needed arsenious oxide to bring about the desired reaction. Secondly, he wanted to make a crystal of arsenious oxide and sulphur for his wireless set. He had previously made a crystal of lead sulphite, but it was no good.

The quantity of arsenic that he required was 2 ounces (875 grains) but that was too much to obtain from an ordinary retail chemist, and it occurred to him that he might be able to get it through the garage, Liddle and Johnston's, from the wholesale chemist, Baird's. He made a telephone enquiry and was told that 2 ounces was too small a quantity to supply to the garage, but that 1lb (7,000 grains) could be made available. It was a simple matter to fill in one of the garage's order forms. He did not bother to initial the order, because he expected that he would have to sign the poisons books personally when he collected the arsenic. (This does not seem to have been the case.)

He did not think it necessary, the explanation continued, to tell anyone connected with the garage that he had ordered in some arsenic, because he thought that an invoice would be sent. (Indeed, that had been duly done, and the account had not been paid.) He was *not* wearing his suit of blue dungarees (which would have made him look like a garage employee) when he collected the arsenic, whatever the assistant at Baird's had said to the police to the contrary.

The 1lb parcel of arsenic was wrapped in brown paper, which he took off. The inner wrapping of white paper was labelled POISON. He put the packet in his left-hip trouser-pocket, where his mother came across it the following morning, as she went through his pockets. (This was theoretically the 'What trash is this?' incident, attested to by Alexis, and by Mr King, although the latter used milder language – 'Willie, is this some more chemicals or stuff that you have been buying?'). Mother told him to put it in the outhouse and took it downstairs herself. *He forgot all about it* (although he had been to such pains to obtain it) and did not know where she had put it. He could only explain his failure of memory by the fact that he had other things to think of. He was so absolutely nervous at having the police about that he forgot to tell them about the arsenic. He thought anyone in a similar position would be in a nervous state. Anyway, he did remember about the packet on Monday June 2nd, when he looked for it and happened to notice it on the pantry shelf. (His mother would surely have seen the POISON label and been more careful or perhaps she was inured to his chemicals.) It was sort of hidden (that was the implication) in the right angle formed by the first shelf and the sliding door of the pantry press. A little of the contents had run out – one of the corners was 'kind of burst'. He first learned of the leakage in his pocket much later, at the police station.

When he found the packet, he thought that he had better take what he required (surely he was not even contemplating chemical experiments three days after Mother's death?) and throw the rest away, because he knew it was so dangerous. The only bottle that was available at the time was the small one labelled 'Potass. Ferricyanide.' and he filled it with about 2 ounces of the arsenic. He never thought of taking the POISON label off the packet, and putting it on the bottle for reasons of safety. Then he put it in his grey jacket pocket. He poured the remainder of the contents of the packet down the pantry sink (in which he had been sick) and threw the wrapper in the fire.

William Laurie King was put to his trial at the High Court of Justiciary in Edinburgh on August 26th 1924. He pleaded Not Guilty. The fifteen jurors, five of whom were women, liked him. He was a golden boy, blond and rosy-cheeked, and he was sturdy, more like a son of the manse, a Boy Scout, than a scheming murderer riddled with hatred and resentment. The judge did not like him at all and made some remarks calculated to cut to the quick. He said this was a young man of no moral character, no moral courage, prone to resort to cowardly expedients and incapable of facing up to unpleasant situations. Father and Alexis, called by the Crown, consistently maintained that there had been no hatred, only love, behind the walls at Wester Coates Terrace. This must have weighed with the jury, as must his father and brother's insistence that William had had no opportunity to add poison to food at the fatal supper. He had not left the room during the whole evening (i.e. to tamper with the food waiting in the pantry), they said, and he had not, definitely not, had the opportunity to sprinkle arsenic on the slices of bread as he cut them. There had, it was true, been a moment when Alexis had stretched across the table between William and his father, but they did not accept that this was sufficient opportunity for the notional sleight of hand. William did not do it.

The defence favoured the theory that the *cheese* had become contaminated by the arsenic, accidentally, on the pantry shelf, even though William, giving evidence, floated the idea that the spilled arsenic was lying on the shelf on which the stale *bread* (i.e. that left over from tea-time) was put when taken out of the crock.

The Crown suggested that there had been no intent to harm Mrs King. The meaning here is that only Father's slice of bread was (lavishly) poisoned. It was sheer bad luck that Mother snaffled his rejected half-slice. This theory then requires that William sat mute and let her eat it. The judge would say, perhaps, that such was his character. Or could the boy, if wickedly inclined, have thought, 'So what?' In the alternative, Mother's first, whole slice was poisoned, too, and she increased the dose by taking Father's. In that case, why did she not, too, complain about the taste?

Arsenic is, famously, a tasteless poison. Why should Mr King have said that the cheese (put on the slice of bread) burned his throat? Judging by the chemical analysis of Mrs King's organs, a large quantity of arsenic was ingested. Taylor's *Medical Jurisprudence* states that in cases where a large quantity has been taken, the powder is described as having a roughish or bitter taste. This is not the same as burning. Dry or burning feeling about the mouth is one of the first symptoms of arsenical poisoning, and that might have been what Mr King was experiencing.

The defence made the rather good suggestion that William might have contaminated the food accidentally by first putting his hand in his pocket, but the Dean of Faculty, for the accused, was shot down in flames by Professor Harvey Littlejohn, who opined that such a route would not bring up enough arsenic to poison anybody. (If his hand had been wet, might he have dredged up more? Could he have sneezed, wiped his mouth or his eyes, or touched coffee?) Much was made of the failure to obtain medical help at the right time, but this was not adequately proved. Even the judge allowed that young people were habitually unobservant, especially of symptoms of illness.

The Crown ridiculed William's explanation for his acquisition of arsenic. Dr Drinkwater, who had analysed various items taken from the Kings' house, stated that he had never heard of the use of arsenic for wireless. (Some readers might know better?) It was very difficult to make crystals from arsenious oxide (and therefore a challenge to William King, perhaps!) and the crystal thus produced was no bigger than a millet seed, and far too small.

As for photography, Dr Drinkwater went on, arsenic had no use in that field. Using arsenic for the purpose of making a magenta dye was 'quite beyond the scope of an amateur'. As we have seen, however, and the opinion was already in evidence in cross-examination, a practising chemist had said that William knew more than he did. It appears that magenta dyes were used routinely in colour photography, but, against William, Taylor says that *arsenates* (salts of arsenic acid) were used in the manufacture of magenta colour, i.e. not white arsenic.

Ferricyanide was a part of the colour process in photography. We know that William had in his possession a bottle which had once (presumably) contained ferricyanide, and it is reasonable to assume that it had been used in photography. Potassium ferricyanide (as on the label) or red prussiate of potash, is formed of dark red crystals, and it was, therefore, guileless to place white arsenic in the bottle. There was no attempt to disguise arsenic as something else. It is not patent from the report available that the defence put up a spirited reply to Dr Drinkwater, but the jury believed William anyway.

The learned judge summed up largely for the defendant, in spite of his reservations as to his moral character, which, he felt, explained many features of William King's actions and explanations. He referred to the absence of motive (since the conflict over his career had been resolved). There was the absence of opportunity to administer the poison. (He obviously did not go with the 'sleight of hand' suggestion.) It was, also, a very serious point that the lad, according to the evidence, himself suffered from sickness. (Perhaps, but there was no evidence that he was seriously ill, nor that he had eaten less bread than his parents.)

If he had intended murder, the judge continued, why would he have left a bottle containing the article that would convict him, in his jacket hanging openly in his bedroom? That was a very difficult fact to square with guilt.

Loud applause greeted the unanimous verdict of Not Guilty and William King returned to his motherless family. Did he abandon chemistry, raze his miniature laboratory to the ground, and embrace his father's profession, in an attempt to make amends for the accident?

CHAPTER 5
THE RUNNING GIRL

girl, running. That is the emblem of the Christina Gilmour case. The fair girl running, running, in the home-fields by night in the autumn of 1842, heavy skirts bunched, one arm awkward, slightly crippled. She was in no danger at all, for no-one was chasing her. Her condition was, in fact, sexual frustration, or, to use that favourite Victorian euphemism, unrequited love. And so, restless, agitated and depressed, trying to relieve the tension, and sending out a message of her desolation, she floundered through mud and frost. Once she had feared the dark, but now her need for one man, and her repudiation of another, drove her out of the house when she should have slept.

This was dairy country, in Ayrshire, where Christina's father, Alexander Cochran, farmed at South Grange, Dunlop. The family had a long tradition of cheese-making, a circumstance oft mentioned by chroniclers, but tenuous to connect with the unco events which were to ensue. Christina was the eldest daughter, born on November 16th 1818, the year when *Northanger Abbey* and *Persuasion* were published. She was pretty and cheerful, and great things were expected of her. They sent her to boarding-schools and a dressmaking establishment in Paisley and Glasgow. It is a pity to disappoint the keen diagnostician, but the slightly impaired right arm, which she could not raise to her head, appears to have been present long before 1842, and was not, therefore, a hysterical conversion symptom.

The focus of all this wasted love was one John Anderson, ten years her senior, whose father farmed at Broadley, about one mile away. They had known each other since childhood, when she had attended classes at the parish school, which was held in a house belonging to his father. There was an understanding, but it must be said that John Anderson was not a strong believer in the doctrine enshrined in the motto that *amor vincit omnia*. The received version of events was to the effect that he had delayed marriage because he was not in a fit financial position to support a wife, but when a rival appeared, he simply caved in, and Christina was left, for all he cared, like Andromeda chained to a rock.

There is no doubt that her parents were to blame. Alexander Cochran was a strict authoritarian, of his class and of his time. He approved of John Gilmour, a better match, younger, too, who farmed on his own account at Town of Inchinnan, near Renfrew. Ardently Gilmour wooed, 'passionate and irrepressible', and when Christina drew back, he threatened suicide – an unhealthy element in the case, and not without its repercussions. The story is that no-one told him about John Anderson, who continued to visit Christina at the cheese farm. One day, she gambled, and lost, by revealing to Anderson that she was engaged to Gilmour. Anderson's only hope now, and Christina's, was an elopement, but he was no Robert Browning, and did the gentlemanly thing, and freed her.

This was when Christina became ill, but her morbid state was not recognised as such. There are old photographs of inmates of Victorian asylums, and they include victims of 'disappointed love', defeated women with their mouths drawn down, their eyebrows crinkled: sometimes they did get better. Christina belonged with them, being looked after, for her own safety, and the safety of others. Father would not confront the truth, even when she began to eat voraciously, to gorge, and her mother had to set limits to her diet. Like a lamb, she was led off to choose her wedding dress. Twice there had to be a postponement, and finally, on November 29th, 1842, the marriage took place, and the new Mrs Gilmour was installed in her matrimonial home, the lonely farm, Town of Inchinnan. The minister, Mathew Dickie, who performed the ceremony, perceived nothing unusual in the bride's demeanour, but then, if she had cried, he would have thought nothing of it.

The marriage was a nullity. Christina sat up in a chair by the fireside on the first night, and it was said that she never undressed during the short term of the marriage. Gilmour did not force her, to his lasting credit, and he did not know, at least at first, that she was pining for another John. During these stressful days, one would not have been surprised to hear that he again threatened suicide.

A curious incident was afterwards reported, to the effect that the newly-married couple, keeping up appearances, visited some neighbours and while they were there, Christina fell into a 'stupor' from which she recovered with a 'sort of epileptic start'. There is no other suggestion that she was an epileptic, and here there is, indeed, a strong intimation of hysteria.

It must not be thought that the unjoined couple lived in frigid isolation. Christina's sisters visited by relay to cheer and assist. By some quaint old custom, the guest dined in the kitchen while her host and hostess ate their meal in uncomfortable gloom in the parlour. There was one living-in maid, Mary Paterson, an old family servant of the Gilmours, who soon found herself the confidante of Christina's lament that she had married John Gilmour against her will, and only because it was the wish of her father: she had intended to take John Anderson. Outside, several men were employed about the farm, and they were loyal to their master.

The first Christmas at Town of Inchinnan was a mere counterfeit of goodwill as Christina presided over the festive fare and Yule logs crackled in the family hearth. Christmas causes emotional upset, confrontation, divorce. People resolve, reject, and scheme. On Boxing Day, all cooking done, Mary Paterson was given leave to visit her sister in Dunlop. Christina gave her some complicated instructions for an unusual errand: on her way, she was to call in at a certain house in Paisley and ask the people there to send out a boy with twopence (supplied) to buy arsenic for rats.

The subterfuge went wrong, however, because the maid forgot the address of the house in Paisley (and would they really have done what was to be asked of them?) and on her way back on December 27th, obligingly bought the arsenic direct from Dr Vessey's chemist's shop in Paisley. She had to say that it was expressly for Mrs Gilmour of Inchinnan. The following afternoon, Christina enacted a charade, a damage limitation, in the outside boiling-house. While she had the attention of Mary Paterson, she threw a paper into the fire, which looked exactly like the arsenic package, saying that it was no use to her, and that she was afraid that she would not be able to use it properly.

Sharp and sudden the next evening, Thursday December 29th, John Gilmour's illness began, and dragged on, with remissions, until January 11th. His symptoms were of a repeated 'throwing' of a 'kind of brownish stuff', pains in the chest and abdomen, and a swelling of the face. Yet he lived, a strong young farmer of 30, and staggered from barn to byre, in and out of bed.

At the New Year, the sick man was hoisted into a gig for a visit to his parents and parents-in-law. While away from home, he vomited, more than once, and was ill in bed back at his farm on January 3rd. The next day, a farm-hand, John Muir, saw him in the stables, his face swollen and his eyes watering. That was the last day on which he walked his land and saw to his men and beasts. Yet still he lived.

On January 6th, Christina Gilmour (who is becoming, as we proceed, a character less and less sympathetic) left home early, telling Mary Paterson that she was going to Renfrew to fetch something for her husband. The farm workers were not to be told. She returned soon after breakfast. As she went into the house, she deposited, or accidentally lost, by reason of unconscious motivation, an incriminating object which John Muir noticed at the corner of the boiling-house, as he came out from breakfast. It had not been there when he went in, and it was not carefully hidden. The strange find was a black silk bag containing a small phial of dark-brownish liquid with a sweet smell, like perfume, and a small paper parcel labelled POISON.

This incident is inexplicable unless seen as another message of distress from inside the mind of Christina Gilmour. You do not lightly lose something which you have obtained secretly, and which fills your thoughts. The farmhouse would have offered safer nooks and crannies for concealment. John Muir took the bag to Mary Paterson (who, incidentally, could not read) and she, in turn, offered it to her mistress. Christina said that she had got some turpentine to rub John with, and went off with the bag.

There was, later, no organised search of modern type for the supplying chemist of the contents of the black silk bag and he was never traced. The packet may be presumed to have been arsenic for rats. Mary Paterson said that it looked like the previous one which she had bought in Paisley. The phial has aroused little comment. There can be only speculation about it. John Muir said that the liquid did not smell like turpentine. Oil of turpentine is colourless, anyway. It could have been genuine perfume bought as a cover and a reassurance to the chemist. Cyanide, with its well-known odour of bitter almonds springs to mind, but prussic acid, too, is like water in appearance. The suspicion must be that Christina obtained a small amount of some other unidentified deadly poison, as much as she could get, on some pretext, in order to top up the arsenic.

That night, Christina went out again, on a public relations exercise, taking with her as witness to her solicitude a farmhand named Sandy Muir. She informed him that, as the master refused to see a doctor (a proposition dubious in itself) she was going to consult her uncle, Robert Robertson, at Paisley. Since that gentleman had not seen his niece for four years, and scarcely recognised her, her choice of adviser was somewhat artificial. She did not turn to her own parents, but to someone removed, not likely to interfere. He did offer to send over his own medical man, Dr McKechnie, but she temporised, saying that she would be happier if her uncle would make a visit first, to see if her husband would agree. She did confide in him the unhappy truth (as she had done to her maid) that she was in a situation not of her own choosing, and that she had really preferred John Anderson. The uncle launched like a parson into a mini-homily on the sacred duties of marriage, concluding with the realistic reflection that many folk had not got the one they liked best. Christina received this wisdom meekly.

Meanwhile, back at the Town of Inchinnan, John Muir was feeling suspicious about the black silk bag, and he went in cautiously to see his master, who was alone and in great pain. 'Jock,' said he to John Muir, '*this is an unco thing!*' These words would appear to be the very epitome of the plight of the poisoned husband on his death-bed. With permission, John Muir, and a lad, set off to fetch a Dr McLaws, of Renfrew, but it was a poor choice of medico, because, not to put too fine a point on it, he was drunk. They met him by chance at Inchinnan Tollhouse at nearly midnight. Christina, returned from her uncle to find the doctor's horse at the door, attended the bibulous consultation, which was singularly ineffectual. No-one (he said) told him that there had been vomiting, and he diagnosed 'inflammation', bleeding the patient with an unsteady hand, horribly to relate, and ordering him to be rubbed with turpentine, as so cleverly prognosticated by the attentive wife.

Next morning, a Saturday, early again, after a bad night, at 8 o'clock, Christina acquired a third remedy for her unhappiness. This time, as she must have done on her second sortie, she proceeded under a false name, telling Alexander Wylie, druggist of Renfrew, that she required arsenic for rats in the field. She was 'Miss Robertson' acting on behalf of a farmer named John Ferguson, but as she was a newcomer to the district, she regretfully could not remember the name of his farm. The oldest local inhabitant, brought in to advise on all possible farms by the slightly suspicious chemist nearly scuppered her, but her mild and fetching manner prevailed.

On the Sunday, Dr Robert McKechnie, the uncle's choice, was called in, and found the patient very feverish, with a pulse of 112, and extremely thirsty. As so often in these poison cases, his diagnosis was of a bilious condition, and he prescribed accordingly – calomel, tartaric acid, soda powders, and a blister. John Muir kept quiet about the black silk bag. The uncle, making up for four years' distance, acted as night-nurse to relieve the exhausted wife. Christina again confided in him her aversion to her marriage, and seemed to be 'brooding' about it. It is as if she would have relented (although it was surely too late) if the uncle – a relative in a position of authority – had said that he understood her pain, and released her.

The doctor asked for vomit and excreta to be preserved for his inspection, but Christina evaded his request. By now, John Gilmour was fast slipping away, and relatives and servants were constantly at his bedside. His wife helped to administer the prescribed powders. He begged to be 'opened' – an ambiguous request. They heard him utter two statements, almost dying declarations: 'Oh, that woman! If you have given me anything...' and 'Oh, if you have given me anything, tell me before I die!' The doctor's son, who assisted his father, found the patient 'very low' on Wednesday the 11th, and bled him – a further insult to his system.

John Gilmour passed away on that day, January 11th, 1843, and he was buried in the churchyard at Dunlop on the 16th, a childless man in his prime, his fields unworked. Christina was a widow in a house which she had never cherished. John Anderson wrote to her. After a couple of months, she went home to her parents, surely hopeful of the attentions of the right John, but he was as laggardly as ever. Gossip followed her like a snuffling hound. Servants talked. After family conferences, Alexander Cochran again intervened with a heavy hand and his customary poor judgement, and arranged to ship his daughter to America, against her will. She objected, saying that flight would be seen as guilt.

On April 21st, the Sheriff granted a warrant for the apprehension of Christina Gilmour, and the exhumation of her husband's body. On the 22nd, the coffin was lifted and a post-mortem was performed immediately, followed by a chemical analysis. Professor Christison later confirmed their findings: there was arsenic in the stomach and in the liver (which was only the second instance at that time of arsenic being detected in the liver). A striking feature of the examination was the fact that the intestines were stained with spots and streaks of a bright yellow colour and the internal surface of the stomach was thickly sprinkled with small yellow particles. On a sweep through six comparable cases, the author has not found a report of yellow colouring, but there clearly is no mystery, because Taylor states that white arsenic can be seen converted into the yellow sulphide of arsenic in the stomach and small intestine, especially when decomposition has begun.

The police arrived at the Cochran farm on April 24th, to execute the warrant, but Christina was already on her way to being smuggled out of the country. The family stoutly denied all knowledge of her whereabouts, themselves committing all manner of auxiliary criminal acts, which were never brought home to them. On the 28th, she wrote to John Anderson from Liverpool. Her family destroyed the letter, and denied the Laodicean lover's recollection that she told him that she would confess to having bought arsenic to take herself, but that she would not admit to having given any to her husband.

Christina Gilmour's escape has the dramatic, episodic quality of an 18th-century picaresque novel. She did not even know her destination, virtually kidnapped, like some beleaguered Clarissa, if not so pure in heart. She left home secretly on foot, banished, although embraced, in the charge of a man whom she did not know, and at a given place was handed over to another stranger, who drove her in a gig to a safe-house, where she was transferred to a third man, with whom she travelled by rail to Liverpool. She may have known the third man, named Simpson, who was a gardener or a shoemaker, and she did not like him at all. He was going to America and had agreed to take Christina with him under the assumed personae of Mr and Mrs John Spiers. The comparison with Crippen and Ethel le Neve is almost too obvious to state. Simpson proved, unlike John Anderson, to be anything but a perfect gentleman, for, intoxicated by the excitement of the situation, he sought to take advantage of his supposed wife (a dangerous ambition) and she had to appeal to the captain for protection. That was Christina's story, and it does not entirely ring true other than in its psycho-sexual sense: she would not have wished to reveal to the captain the sham of her identity.

It did not matter, anyway, because as their packet-ship *Excel* bounced and dipped across the Atlantic, Superintendent McKay, armed with a new warrant was in pursuit aboard the much faster, picturesque, Cunard paddle-steamer *Arcadia*, and Christina was arrested off Staten Island. McKay recognised her from a previous encounter, depleted and ravaged as she was by sea-sickness and the strain of fighting off the advances of Simpson the shoemaker. A treaty for extradition in such cases was just in place, and proceedings were brought in June before United States Commissioner, named Sylvanus Rapalyea. Thomas Warner, of the New York Bar, tried every angle to defeat the treaty. Christina was quite sane enough to feign insanity, but she had led a sheltered life and her play-acting would not have fooled any doctor worth his salt. She sat on the floor like a pixie, cut her hands with scissors, said that she liked to see the flies licking up the blood, and saw her grandmother lying on her bed in her holding-cell. She also expressed a preference for going home in a coach, rather than a ship, but perhaps she intended an irony.

All pleas having failed, Christina's passage to Scotland on the packet *Liverpool* was not a smooth one, and there was time for reflection. At night, she was locked in her cabin with an unofficial wardress (just as a real lunatic would have been) while McKay kept guard outside. Back at Paisley, she made a judicial declaration before the Sheriff, and what she said was wily and to the point, with lies and distortions. There was an implication that her husband might have committed suicide: 'He said to me shortly before his death that I had broken his heart. I suppose that he said this because I told him often before that he had broken mine and that I could not be to him as a wife.'

She sought to reduce her acquisitions of arsenic from three to two, admitting the arsenic for rats, which she burnt in front of Mary Paterson, without, she said, ever opening the packet, and owning to the black silk bag incident, which she deliberately fused with the third, known purchase from Wylie the chemist. She 'rather thought' that she dropped the bag. The purpose of this poison was her own suicide, because she felt that they were all tired of her and would not let her have peace. She did not take it, but kept it in her pocket until the string came off the paper and some of the contents were spilt. There it stayed, until she discovered it after Gilmour's death, when she had gone home to her parents. Her mother took possession of it.

The trial of Christina Gilmour, in Edinburgh, began on January 12th 1844. Like all those Victorian women accused of murdering their husbands, she provided an interesting spectacle in her black dress and veil, forbidden at that time to speak, and held to the words of her declaration. The defence freely conceded that John Gilmour had died of arsenical poisoning, but argued that, grieved by the state of the marriage, he had killed himself. In the alternative, he had poisoned himself by accident. His actual possession of arsenic, kept as a rodenticide, was neatly proved by the evidence of Mary Paterson that he had moved the 'kist' or chest which contained his stock of the poison into the bedroom, from the kitchen, on the occasion of his marriage. There it was, available for him to rifle when he felt the suicidal urge, or to use clumsily against the rats. No explanation was given for the transference from kitchen to bedroom. Perhaps he felt that with the kitchen in proper use, there might be a mistake. He must have kept the kist locked, or why would Christina have travelled for miles in search of arsenic? Why did she not, theoretically, ask him to dole out some rat poison for her to use?

A broken heart, said Counsel for Christina, might lead to suicide, but not to murder and, in spite of the strong circumstantial evidence, the corporate mind of the jury revolted from the notion of the guilt of one of so 'very gentle, mild, fine disposition' (John Anderson's words) who had held her husband's head when he vomited. Arsenic is a cruel agent of death – and we now know that it is carcinogenic, should a person survive its administration – and Not Proven was, in the circumstances, a kind verdict.

Christina Gilmour went home to her mother and father. John Anderson did not marry her. She had no taste for greater adventure, for those travels abroad so popular with beneficiaries of the Not Proven verdict, but lived quietly, and turned to the Church. She died on December 14th 1905, at the age of 87, and her last known place of residence was Stewarton, in Ayrshire, unless, of course, someone has better knowledge.

CHAPTER 6
THE TRAVELLING MAN

In a drear, wast place, they found the body of the travelling man, hidden in the waters of the bleak tarn named Loch Tor-na-Eigin, in the parish of Assynt, a part of that highest north-west region, maritime on its serrated edges, which lies 30 miles below Cape Wrath.

The itinerant merchant, a strong man walking, burdened with a heavy pack of wares, his humped figure seen in silhouette toiling over passes to distant villages, was once a vital part of the economy of the Highlands. It was a calling of some antiquity. Scott's character, Bryce Snailsfoot, a pedlar active in the Northern Isles in *The Pirate*, came from times around 1700. Romantic and colourful as these old trades seem to us now, they must have been arduous and uncomfortable in the extreme. One thinks of Hardy's reddleman in *The Return of the Native*, saturated with red ochre in every pore. Men of solitary disposition may have been attracted to such ways of life.

The peril for the packman, travelling alone with his stave like a pilgrim but with, it is to be hoped, some kind of weaponry to defend himself, was that the mere sight of him was an allurement to villainy. A moving target, he carried often valuable materials, and, as his pack lightened, a growing store of real money. Murdoch Grant's pack contained linens, silk handkerchiefs, prints, cottons, and worsted stockings. These were goods of quality. Another traveller could just as well have peddled pots and pans, ribbons and beads, and pins and needles.

A decent young man of 25, Murdoch Grant was based at Strathbeg, in Lochbroom, Ross-shire, and his beat covered parts of Sutherland, Ross and Cromarty. Who knows how many business rivals he had, but he was doing well, because when he left home for Assynt, in March, 1830, he valued his goods for sale at £40. He was a guest at the wedding of a girl called Betty Fraser on March 11th, and that occasion was good for trade. For one week before his disappearance on March 19th, he stayed in the Assynt district, being put up in the homes of several of his customers, which is a measure of his blameless character.

He was last seen alive on the road to Nedd, homeward-bound for St Patrick's market at Strathbeg. No-one missed him – he was a bachelor – because he was a travelling man, but he did, in fact, have an appointment in Lynmeanach, with a certain Hugh Macleod, a young schoolmaster.

It is no anachronism to look back and see things as they were, and realise that Macleod was a psychopath even if the term were not then in use. His abnormality of mind caused him to commit a truly terrible crime, not accountable by saying that he was 'spoilt' by his parents and pushed beyond his station in life. He was a lost creature of no judgement and less conscience. Although he had come, trailing clouds of glory, 20 years before, to his parents' croft at Lynmeanach, he had repaid their devotion with bad behaviour.

The Scottish Enlightenment had spread the idea of the importance of education and culture and 'the humble crofter' in the Highlands had heard the new voices. Hugh's father, Roderick, a tenant farmer, was determined to educate his only son to a higher standard than would have been expected. He was obviously an interesting man in his own right, first teaching Hugh at home, and then engaging a tutor, since there was no school near enough in that remote part of Assynt. Later, a school did open but, to contribute to the expenses of his education, the boy was placed for some time as a shepherd with a neighbouring farmer.

This is when he is supposed to have gone astray, to have been corrupted by the rough farm lads, a wild lot, who introduced him to girls, whisky, gambling at cards, swearing, and, most heinously, training sheep-dogs on the Sabbath. So far, so good, none of this made him a psychopath, but a hint, a whisper of something that was to cause trouble shows in his excessive need for, in his own words, 'pretty dress'. He began to incur debts, and angry, forsaken maidens pursued him, but, surprisingly, his reputation in general was still good and he was *persona grata*, an admired, improved and polished young man at all the social gatherings.

In 1828, he was appointed assistant-schoolmaster at Coigarth, in Lochbroom, an achievement in itself, but the salary did not provide the peacock with his feathers, and teacher turned burglar without a qualm. In the June of that year, he broke into a shop in Lochbroom, emptied the till, and stole a whole web of tweed, which he hid under a cairn of stones until the winter, when he had the good cloth made up into a new suit, explaining that he had bought it from a travelling merchant. No-one suspected the schoolmaster. He is beginning to earn the label of psychopath. One Sunday, he absented himself from church, saying that his shoes needed repairing, and coolly let himself into a neighbour's empty house, opened a chest with his own keys and stole his nest egg.

The peacock was insatiable in his desire for fresh plumage, and he began to ruminate in a bloodthirsty way about those peripatetic pedlars. By 1830, he was back living with his parents, and teaching at the school at Nedd. In the late afternoon, coming home from school with a pupil, Donald Wilson, he addressed him strangely.

'We are poor, Donald,' said he, 'and there are plenty of travelling merchants here about. Though we should kill one of them and take his money [note the scholarly syntax] there would be no harm.'

'But we could not do that without being found out,' said Wilson.

'Would you tell?' Hugh said. 'For if you would not tell, we could do it easily enough.'

'Oh, Hugh, Hugh! Though I should conceal it, God would not.' The schoolmaster changed the subject, but in his mind he had formed the resolution to kill Murdoch Grant, for they were probably already well acquainted and Grant carried the very treasures most desired: clothing and money.

On the road to Nedd, he lay in wait for his prey. It was Thursday March 18th. He had a plan. There was to be no risky scene where others might pass. It was a friendly meeting and first the two nice-looking young men, in the prime of life, went to Widow Mackay's house where the merchant bought some worsted stockings. Before they parted, they had arranged to meet again on the following day, when they would go to Hugh's home at Lynmeanach and Hugh would buy the entire contents of his pack. It was to be a secret.

Before breakfast, the next morning, the schoolmaster went out to the barn, and knelt down and prayed for God's blessing on his enterprise. Casting about for a weapon, he selected a large, wedge-shaped mason's hammer (of the type used, no doubt, by Hardy's Jude the Obscure) and shortened the handle, to make it more portable. This is all textbook premeditation, and it would be very difficult to gloss over, or, really, to mitigate in the modern sense, his horrendous actions. After supping his porridge, he put on his father's greatcoat to conceal the hammer, and set off for the road to Nedd.

The appointment was for noon and the weather was not good, so he sat in a cave, like the apocryphal anthropophagous Sawney Beane, and waited until the pedlar arrived. They walked in the direction of Nedd. When they reached a cemetery, Grant sat down on a grave to rest, his burden being heavy, but the symbolism of the scene was lost on the schoolmaster and he was in no mind to relent. Leaving the road, they struck off across moorland, Hugh sometimes helping out by carrying the pack. Several times he steeled himself to strike the fatal blow, but he was afraid that someone might be watching from the hills.

'At length we got near Loch Tor-na-Eigin,' he later confessed. 'I was going first. I suddenly turned round, and with a violent blow under the ear felled him to the ground. I took the money out of his warm pocket, and put it into mine. There was about £9 in all. I dragged the body into the loch, as far as I could with safety to myself. It was evening, but not very dark. I then threw the hammer into the loch, and returned and rifled the pack. I took the most portable things, and sunk the heavy goods in a moss loch [peat bog] further into the moor. After taking the money from the pocket-book, I buried it on the edge of a bank near where the body was thrown.'

It was noticed in the following weeks that the schoolmaster, previously indigent, was shelling out freely from a red pocket-book. He paid up his debts, bought whisky and new clothes, a gun for 32 shillings, and was generous with his friends. Day after day, on his way to and from the school at Nedd, he passed the tainted loch without a shudder, concerned only to judge the water level as spring advanced. He was, as always, conducting his affairs with safety to himself.

The waters of the tarn were deep and the banks sloped steeply. Without a boat he had not been able to sink the body in the centre. The level receded a little, until he could actually see the body where it lay upon the moss beneath the bank. He was afraid to move it, even at night. One month after the murder, the once pure tarn managed to rid itself of its secret. Down in its glassy depths, unusually low and limpid, the sharp eyes of a boy, John Mackenzie, of Drumbeg, saw the shape, like a long, still, dark fish.

When the body was beached, it was found that the antiseptic properties of the cushioning moss had delayed decomposition. A group of 50 people drawn from the scattered crofts and hamlets gathered at the waterside, and one man present was able to identify Murdoch Grant. His pack, almost a part of him, was suspiciously missing. His pockets were turned inside out. The schoolmaster was there, contributing to the speculation, and it was noticed that he alone did not acknowledge the ancient ordeal of *Bahr-recht* (Law of the Bier) which was founded on the belief that the corpse would bleed at the touch of the murderer. Detached, he stood back, as the others stooped, and they respected his better education.

It was put to him that he was the right messenger to undertake the six-mile walk to the manse to report the death to the minister and arrange a burial. The schoolmaster said that he did not like travelling alone in the dark, and a lad named Donald Graham was deputed to walk with him. Another of those pregnant conversations took place. Donald, revelling in the drama, remarked that he hoped that they would not be suspected, living, as they did, so near to the loch. Hugh halted and looked straight at his companion: 'Do you think that I would do it?'

At the manse, the Reverend Mr Gordon asked some questions. Hugh said that it was a drowned body, and that it bore 'scratches' from knocking against the rocks. It was an accident or a suicide. It was by now too late for any action, and back at Tor-na-Eigin, the body was re-consigned to the water, to keep it fresh overnight – like a salmon. Next morning, early, with the minister in attendance, a grave was dug beside the loch, the body was retrieved and buried in a coffin which had been carried to the scene. From the heights of a nearby hill, Hugh Macleod, who was supposed to have overslept, was observed, dodging about like a wary deer, to watch the obsequies.

These dubious proceedings pleased not the procurator fiscal, and the restless body of the travelling man was, on April 29th, exhumed for an alfresco post-mortem at the spot under the gaze of spectators. The schoolmaster gave all possible assistance towards the logistics of the event, having been warmly recommended to the Sheriff by the minister as a reliable figure of some authority in the district. He who had feared to walk alone by night now watched the surgeons at their task without a quiver, although it did cross his mind, in a precognitive flash, that he himself might one day be the subject of a similar autopsy.

The examining doctors, both local surgeons, found that injuries to the head, inflicted probably by a hammer, were the cause of death. The schoolmaster acted as interpreter at the Sheriff's inquiry, knowing the Gaelic tongue and familiar with the ways of the local inhabitants. He was very plausible, and extremely well-dressed. Village gossip, however, betrayed him: the postmaster intimated to the Sheriff that his lay-helper, the eager schoolmaster, had, soon after the supposed date of the murder, asked him for change for a £10 Bank of England note which, by the postmaster's judgement, he had been in no position to hold. Enquiry was made of Hugh Macleod's financial circumstances, and he lied and blustered. Blood on his coat came, he said, from a bird which he had shot with his new gun.

Removed to Dornoch jail, he bought whisky through his cell window, and assured a visiting minister, the Reverend Mr Kennedy, that he was an innocent man. At night, though, his guilty mind played strange tricks: he dreamt that he stood in a cemetery which he had never seen before, watching an old man digging a grave, beside which lay an empty coffin. As the sexton turned towards him, he recognised his father's face. 'Hugh,' said the sexton, 'here is your grave: lie down in it now, for your time is come.' Seized with terror, he pleaded for more time, and the old man relented: 'Well, Hugh, go for this time, but remember that in a year your coffin will meet you. Mark that. Do not forget.'

These were supernatural times; the pure tarn lapped at its banks, and prophesy was in the air. A young journeyman tailor, a friend of the schoolmaster, named Kenneth Fraser and known then or later as 'Kenneth the Dreamer' was, in his turn, visited by a visionary dream. The search for the pedlar's pack had been given up as a hopeless task, but, being fast asleep, Kenneth heard a voice 'like a man's' which spoke to him in Gaelic: 'The pack of the merchant is lying in a cairn of stones in a hollow near their house.' With the vatic words there came a clear vision of the south-west side of Loch Tor-na-Eigin (not then known to the dreamer) with the sun shining on the ground, and 'the burn running beneath Macleod's house.' It was so vivid a dream that he could have been awake.

Nothing was found in the hollow which he had described, but, further up the burnside, certain articles identified as the pedlar's property were uncovered from a hole hidden by stones. In fact, Hugh had hidden the actual pack there, but had later disposed of it elsewhere, leaving those few articles for Kenneth to discover. Whether or not Kenneth had some real, earthly, knowledge, we do not know, but it is worth mentioning that psychic dreams are sometimes approximate in their details.

The trial of Hugh Macleod occupied twenty-four continuous hours at the Circuit Court of Justiciary at Inverness on September 27th 1831. Kenneth the Dreamer made an impressive witness, bardic, and his evidence was sympathetically received. No witnesses were called by the defence. Upon the unanimous verdict of Guilty, the schoolmaster started to his feet and cried, 'The Lord Almighty knows that I am innocent. I didn't think anyone in this country would be condemned on mere opinion.' Unfortunately for him, the importance of circumstantial evidence had been well canvassed during the trial, Lord Moncrieff having referred to the fact that 'cases of this occult and secret nature' were often more satisfactorily proved by indirect evidence than by direct evidence which might possibly be procured by perjury.

The same judge assumed the black cap and sentenced the prisoner to be executed at Inverness on October 24th, between the hours of two and four in the afternoon, and his body was to be given to the Professor of Anatomy in Edinburgh for dissection. Back in his cell, the schoolmaster confessed, and from then until the end his piety knew no bounds. On the appointed day of execution, they walked him in procession to the place called Longman's Grave. He was arrayed in the macabre costume then considered appropriate for the occasion: a long black robe, to the ground, a white nightcap for his bowed head, and a halter round his neck, the end of which was carried behind him by the hangman. The spectacle was medieval and perhaps the 7,000 or 8,000 people who came to watch the execution saw it as a morality play.

Stationed on the scaffold, the schoolmaster surveyed his audience and launched into a long preachment until he dried up, or until they silenced him. 'If I were to live for 100 years,' he vowed, 'never would I put a glass to my head [sic], never would I hold a card in my hand.' And never again would he, in 100 years, open his mouth to a strange woman. Kenneth the Dreamer, he also declared, in a rush of altruism, was entirely innocent of any knowledge of the murder. It was, in fact, proved at the trial that Kenneth had had an alibi for the time of the crime – he was at work all that week – but there was a kind of explanation for the famous dream. He had joined the schoolmaster for drinking bouts, paid for out of the pedlar's red pocket-book, and something might have been let drop, for Hugh was prone to making mysterious remarks, which had lodged in Kenneth's mind.

William Roughead turns most poetically and unforcedly to Sir Thomas Browne for a commentary on dreams – 'The phantasms of sleep do commonly walk in the great road of natural and animal dreams, wherein the thoughts or actions of the day are acted over and echoed in the night.' Let us deepen, or complicate, the idea by invoking Freud (who was certainly not Roughead's bedtime reading) and his distinguishing of the manifest and the latent aspect of dreams. He would have said that Kenneth's famous dream, in its latent meaning, pointed to an issue of a more distant past and of cardinal importance to Kenneth the Dreamer. 'There are,' Freud said, 'no indifferent dream instigators; hence, too, no innocent dreams.'

CHAPTER 7
THE NAKED GHOST

In the heart of the Grampians, in the month of September, 1749, a party of eight men of the 6th Regiment of Foot, which was commanded by Lieutenant General John Guise (described by Horace Walpole as a very brave soldier but a great romancer), were lodged at a small upland farm, Dubrach, near the village of Inverey west of Braemar, some ten miles from Balmoral. They had marched there in June from their regimental headquarters at Aberdeen, and they were under the charge of Sergeant Arthur Davies. Another party of the same regiment, under a corporal, guarded the Spittal of Glenshee, a hamlet at the head of Glenshee, about 12 miles to the south. Twice a week, during their regular patrols, the two sections met halfway, generally showed the flag, and exchanged information.

Lurking and running in the heather, some bands of Jacobites, remnants of the Rising of 1745, survivors of Culloden or sympathisers who feared reprisals, still posed a sufficient threat to the nervous government for the maintenance of garrisons stationed throughout the suspected districts. Apart from their role of encouraging the others, the duty of the military was to enforce (as far as they could) the two Disarming Acts and the banning of the bagpipes as an 'instrument of war'. Additionally by the Dress Act, the wearing of the kilt, plaid, or any tartan garment was proscribed.

Sergeant Davies was a career soldier, anxious to become a sergeant-major, and he was popular with officers and other ranks. The neighbouring Highlanders would have known, to be sure, if he had been tarnished with recent atrocities, and he was regarded as a fair man and well enough accepted considering the equipoise demanded of his charge. A genial personage, he had two characteristics which led inevitably, as it seemed to those who warned him, to his demise. Bluff and fearless, convinced that it would never happen to him, that, as it were, flying was safer than crossing the road, he was a keen sportsman and he would insist on striking off on expeditions of his own with rod and gun, deep into the peopled heather.

As if this were not adequate challenge to fate, he chose to array himself in swellish clothes and to port his valuables dangling from his person. In short, he moved about the wild hills like a royal 12-pointer waiting for the rifle. His wife of twelve months, Jean, who shared his billet and loved him dearly, was proud of his appearance, and he glittered like a Christmas tree indeed with silver baubles.

His ordinary dress was a blue surtout coat, with a striped silk vest, and a silver-laced hat with a silver button. His dark, mouse-coloured hair was tied behind with a black silk ribbon. Large silver shoe-buckles ornamented his brogues, and he had silver buckles at his knees, a silver watch and seal at his fob, two dozen silver buttons on his waistcoat, and two gold rings on his fingers. Lacking the kist or chest of the crofters, he carried a green silk purse which contained his capital of fifteen and a half guineas in gold, and a leather purse with silver for current expenses. The green silk purse was no secret in the district, because he used to jingle it to amuse the local children. An unusual penknife, and a gun with a peculiar barrel given to him by a comrade, comprised his personal armoury.

On Thursday September 28th, the sergeant was out on patrol as usual, combining sport with duty. He left the farm before sunrise, in advance of his men, as he had done before, unorthodox as it sounds. Four of his men followed later. On his way, in Glen Clunie, he reprimanded, but did not arrest, a man named John Growar, who was wearing a tartan coat. Marching to the rendezvous with the corporal's guard from Glenshee, his four men had a distant sighting of their sergeant hunting on the hills, and they heard him fire a shot. They did not see him again. The Glenshee party had encountered him half a mile from the rendezvous, at the Water of Benow. He said that he was going to the hill to get a shot at the deer, and the corporal thought it 'very unreasonable in him' as he himself was nervous even when accompanied by his men. Nonsense, said the sergeant, in characteristic form, when he had his arms and ammunition about him; he feared no-one. Off he went, striding through the heather, silver jewellery glinting, and green silk purse jingling.

Two eye-witnesses saw what happened to Sergeant Davies, but they were fugitives, who had taken to the high ground for political reasons, and they deemed it prudent to move on and say nothing. Angus Cameron, from Rannoch, and Duncan Cameron were waiting for Donald Cameron (who was afterwards hanged) and some other friends from Lochaber. They had spent the previous night on Glenbruar Braes, and they had been hiding all day in a little hollow on the side of the Hill of Galcharn. About noon, they kept quiet as two men with guns passed close by the spot where they were lying. Angus Cameron recognised one of them, wearing a grey plaid with some red in it, as Duncan Terig, alias Clerk, a reputed thief who lived with his father in the village of Inverey, where the sergeant was billeted.

The other man with the gun, not known to the watchers in the heather, was, in fact, Alexander Bain Macdonald, forester to Lord Braco of Kilbryde, first Earl of Fife, and he came from Allanaquoich, a village situated a couple of miles from Inverey. His reputation was none too good either, and the point is that both were local men, who knew things that mattered to them. Five men were on the hill where only one should have been.

An hour or so before sunset, the watchers in the heather, still lying low, saw, in relief against the sky on a mound opposite, about a gunshot away, the bright figure of a man in a blue coat, his hat edged with white or silver lace and a gun in his hand. Coming up the hill towards the stranger, were the two men with guns who had been there in the forenoon. They met at the top and there was some kind of parley. Then Clerk, the thief in the grey and red plaid, struck the man in blue upon the breast, and he, the sergeant, cried out, clapped his hand to his breast, turned his back on the two men and strode away. Brave and tragic, he was outnumbered, and saw for the last time the wild hills of Scotland as the two men shot him in the back. There were two separate reports. They stooped down and 'handled' the body of the fallen sergeant.

That night, the hunter came not home, and the tidings spread throughout the district. A party of men were sent out from the garrison at Braemar Castle to help with the search, but after four days it was abandoned. The wife, Jean, was convinced that the sergeant had been murdered for his money. There was a rumour that he had deserted, but her fine words denied it, 'for that he and she lived together in as great amity and love as any couple could do that ever was married, and that he never was in use to stay away a night from her, and that it was not possible he could be under any temptation to desert, as he was much esteemed and beloved'.

Time passed. It was June of the following year. A young shepherd, Alexander McPherson, was guarding his master's flock by night, asleep, actually, in a sheiling apart from the main farmhouse at Glen Clunie. He woke. An apparition of a man clad in blue, whom he at first took to be a real living man, was standing over him. It drew Alexander outside, away from the other sleepers within. 'I am the ghost of Sergeant Davies,' it intoned, and the lad believed him. They spoke in Gaelic, which was wonderful indeed, since the sergeant had never learnt the language of the people whom he controlled.

The ghost, this fluently Gaelic-speaking ghost, communicated a message and enjoined a mission. It seemed that he had been murdered on the Hill of Christie, and he wanted his bones to be buried in decency. At first Alexander, frightened out of his wits, refused to comply, and the ghost suggested that Donald Farquharson, the son of Michael, with whom the sergeant had lodged, would be willing to help him out. Emboldened, the shepherd enquired who had done the deed, but the ghost made gnomic reply that if he had not asked, he might have told him, and vanished 'in the twinkling of an eye'.

To the Hill of Christie, the shepherd presently made his way, and at the very spot designated by the spectre, found the pitiful bones under a bank, practically reduced to a skeleton. He drew them out with his crook and deposited them in a peat-bog. The mouse-coloured hair was still tied in its black silk ribbon. Fragments of blue cloth and striped silk, and a pair of brogues from which the silver buckles had been cut completed the picture. And there Alexander left the matter, under the maxim of doing nothing if in doubt.

Thwarted, the insistent ghost made a revisitation, one week later, and this time, for greater impact, presumably, it was stark naked although modesty impelled it to bend over. It was night, again, and all should have been sleeping, but Isobel McHardie awoke in the communal hut and saw something naked come in at the door in a bowing posture. She drew the clothes over her head and saw, or heard, no more. Alexander awoke and the naked ghost repeated his request. When pressed again for the name of the murderer, it abandoned its previous reticence and supplied two names – Duncan Clerk and Alexander Macdonald.

Then, at last, the shepherd summoned the chosen one, Donald Farquharson, to the sheiling, told him about the visitation, dealt with his scepticism, and led him to view the sergeant's remains. Convinced, now, Farquharson asked solemnly, or perhaps with his tongue in his cheek, if the ghost had given any orders about conveying the bones to a churchyard. Since no preference had been indicated, they buried all the remains in the peat-bog there and then.

What story the ghost had told was 'clattered' about the

district, and local inhabitants were drawn to the Hill of Christie as if for treasure trove. The sergeant's gun with its distinctive barrel was found, and a girl named Isobel Ego, who was possessed of a remarkable id, came upon his silver-laced hat. She had been sent to the hills to look for some grazing horses, and took home her find, saying that she had come in richer than when she went out. The farmer's wife, however, confiscated it and had no peace of mind until her husband hid it under a stone by the burnside, where children found it and took it to the village. It passed through several hands until it rested with the barrack-master at Braemar Castle.

Yet nothing happened for four years. These were not normal times. No-one wanted to be an informer. There was fear of terrible reprisals. A gallant English soldier serving far from home had been done to death.

Meanwhile, Clerk's circumstances had unaccountably bucked up: he had taken two farms on lease and married Elizabeth Downie, who displayed an unusual gold ring with a little heart bossed upon the bezel which bore a remarkable resemblance to the ring previously worn by Sergeant Davies. Clerk also carried a long green silk purse. He attempted to suborn the shepherd lad, Alexander McPherson, or perhaps that is too strong a term, but he certainly did, after much persuasion, tempt him to enter his employment. One day, when they were up on the hills together, Clerk, 'spying a young cow' told his new shepherd to shoot it. What cruelty, sadism or sport was this? McPherson reacted angrily, saying that it was such thoughts as these that were in his master's mind when he murdered Sergeant Davies. If he had dared, Clerk might have killed him then, but he 'fell calm', begged him to keep the secret, said that he would be as a brother, offered to stock a farm for him, and gave him a promissory note for £20, to hold his tongue. Some time later, when the shepherd approached him, he refused to honour the note, and McPherson left his service, where he could never have been comfortable. After

Clerk's ultimate arrest, his brother Donald solicited the shepherd to leave the country and in the alternative offered him half of what he, Donald, was worth if the shepherd would bear false witness.

It was not until September, 1753, that Clerk and Macdonald were at last accused by the voice of the country, as the Lord Advocate put it, and committed to the Castle of Braemar. Each made contradictory declarations: Clerk, that he and Macdonald were upon another hill at the relevant time, both armed (that he admitted) and that Macdonald fired one shot only at some deer before they parted at 10 o'clock that morning and he himself returned to his father's house. Alexander Macdonald's version was that, after they had separated, he had spent the following night at home in Allanaquoich, and not, as Clerk had said, at Clerk's home. This fundamental discrepancy would have appeared fatal to the accomplices, but we shall see...

On June 11th, 1754, at the High Court of Justiciary in Edinburgh, a jury composed of tradesmen was empanelled. Macdonald was allowed to amend the discrepancy and now remembered that he had spent the night with Clerk in Inverey. It was to be a most peculiar trial. What the naked ghost had said to the shepherd was allowed in evidence by some exception to the general rule against hearsay. The case for the Crown was very strong and included the eye-witness testimony of the two hiders in the heather.

The widow Jean testified that while the search-party for her missing husband was being assembled, she had asked the prisoner Clerk, whom she took to be a particular friend, to try hard to find the body. No doubt she mistook his conspicuous show of concern. Isobel Ego's find, the silver-laced hat, was produced and she identified it by the initials, wrongly placed, as it happened, which she had seen him cut on the outside of the crown. She knew his gun by the cross rent in the middle of the barrel, caused by firing a shot when the gun was overloaded. It emerged that she had been widowed before. David Holland, a paymaster of the same regiment, the sergeant's predecessor, had given her a plain gold ring engraved on the inside with the letters D.H., and the trist motto, 'When this you see, Remember me'. With a typical hearty attitude to life, Sergeant Davies had had no compunction about wearing his comrade's ring, nor yet his silver shoe-buckles, also bearing the initials D.H. The plain ring had long vanished, but the embossed and cordiform one was an important part of the prosecution case. Elizabeth Downie, Clerk's wife, an incompetent witness at his trial, had told varying stories about her rings. Examined by Colonel Forbes, Justice of the Peace, she had said that, before her marriage, she had possessed a *copper* ring, with a round knot of the same material on it, and that she had given it away to a herdsman named Reoch.

Donald Farquharson, who had helped the shepherd to bury the bones, seemed to have a finger in every pie. He had actually been present when the sergeant had overloaded his gun and cracked the barrel. He had seen a gold ring with a knob on it adorning the hand of Elizabeth Downie, and he had questioned her about it. She said that it had belonged to her mother. It was within his personal knowledge that Alexander Macdonald, as forester to Lord Braco, was the only local man who held a warrant for carrying a gun for purposes of shooting deer. He also knew that Clerk usually went with him on shooting trips, and, moreover, Clerk was reputed to be a sheep-stealer. He knew nothing against Alexander Macdonald except that he once broke into the kist of a man called Corbie, and stole his money. He considered the shepherd to be an honest lad, but, he said, it was the general opinion that everything he said could not be relied on. That is, he is repudiating the naked ghost.

Lauchlan McIntosh, servant of the sergeant's landlord, was there to contribute to matters against Alexander Macdonald: two years after the disappearance, he had seen him with a penknife very like the sergeant's, and, when challenged,

Macdonald had said that there were many 'sic-likes' around. Isobel McHardie, who had hidden her head under the bedclothes in the sheiling, corroborated, as it were, the naked ghost. The morning after the haunting, she had spoken to the shepherd, who had assured her that it would not trouble them again.

John Grant, of Altalaat, testified that the two accused men lodged at his house the night before the disappearance, in readiness for a deer-hunting expedition the next day. He saw them set out, after sunrise, Clerk's gun illegal, Macdonald's warranted. He himself was then away for four days at a fair in Kirkmichael, but his son spotted them going up the water to the Hill of Gleney – which was where the accused had declared that they had stayed – about a mile and a half from the Hill of Christie.

Angus Cameron, an unhappy witness, lonely without his fellow watcher in the heather, Duncan Cameron, who had since died from undisclosed causes, perhaps natural, claimed that it was not until the following summer that he had heard by chance about the demise of Sergeant Davies and realised what he had witnessed. He had consulted two Cameron friends who had advised him to say nothing as it might bring him trouble and cause reprisals against the Highlanders.

Evidence for the defence was negligible. Reoch, who should have been there to say that Elizabeth Downie had given him an embossed copper ring failed to turn up, and was fined 100 Scots merks. Heaven knows what happened to him, a herdsman, if he could not find the money.

'All in one voice' the jury found the two accused Not Guilty, a verdict entirely against the weight of the evidence. It was suggested that the jury refused to convict because they were of Jacobite persuasion and would not have mourned the passing of a member of the English force. Against this theory, however, was the thought that those in trade were not in general of rebellious disposition, because they had come to benefit from the Act of Union of 1707. There must be an explanation for the verdict – probably the whole of Scotland knew what it was at the time – but it is now obscure. Sheer patriotism after Culloden may have been the reason for sparing a pair of robbers, the particular subsumed in the larger statement. As for the ghost, Isobel McHardie did see something. It was the opinion of Sir Walter Scott that the shepherd had learnt of the identity of the murderers by ordinary means (and indeed in that close-knit community there seems to have been little privacy) and invented the entire ghost story so that he would not appear as an informer. In that case, he would have had to persuade a man to appear in a state of nakedness, when at least most persons in the sheiling were asleep (for there were a number) and then he would have had to wake up the woman to witness to the ghost. If all had woken they would have challenged or recognised the naked imposter.

On balance, there probably was a 'ghost' and the shepherd was picked for his credulity and trusting nature, intended to broadcast the truth. There is no evidence that he was simple. He did say that his first impression was that the spectre was a 'real living man', namely one of the Farquharsons, who has not previously appeared in the story, and who was the brother of that Donald Farquharson to whom the shepherd had appealed for help. This was curious and would indicate a public-spirited collusion between the two brothers, with the shepherd as their puppet. The difficulty here is that Donald Farquharson at first refused to believe the shepherd's story and only reluctantly was dragged to the Hill of Christie which in his own words, 'he did the rather that he thought it might possibly be true, and if it was, he did not know but that the apparition might trouble himself.' Considerable cunning would attach to such an attitude, but then, unless naked ghosts caper freely through Scottish folklore the effrontery of the vision stands out and betrays an original mind.

CHAPTER 8
THE CINDERELLA SYNDROME

The radix of Bertie Willox's crime – parricide, the unnatural act, against nature, *à rebours* – surely lay in the oppressive domestic circumstances which trapped the boy without future prospects in a situation which reversed his gender-identity. Pushed too hard, the case tells us, Cinderella might turn ugly! So complicated were the Oedipal possibilities of the set-up at No 79 Grove Street, that some kind of psycho-dynamic explosion would appear to have been inevitable.

Here, in the poor tenement district of Cowcaddens, Glasgow, Robert Swift Willox lived in isolation with his father, also Robert. An only child (as far as we know) Bertie was born on May 15th 1909, at 122 Cambridge Street. He attended four schools in succession, two Catholic and two Protestant, before starting work at the age of 14. His jobs indicate a desire and aptitude to make a career for himself. Beginning as a message-boy, he was an apprenticed engineer with Messrs A & J Inglis, the firm of shipbuilders for whom his father worked, and then he moved on to Simpson, Lawrence & Co, yacht outfitters, and they paid him the good wage (for his age) of 16 shillings per week.

Robert Willox, *père*, known to Bertie rather pathetically as Dada, was a dark figure, antisocial, unapproachable, but it is possible that his so-called moroseness was a legacy of his war experiences. He was a survivor of Mons and lucky to reach the age of 55. A native of Aberdeen, he was employed there as a young man in some capacity on the staff of a local newspaper until he left in a hurry, and his creditors and his family heard no more of him. He joined the army in 1898 at the age of 24 and served throughout the Boer War in the Royal Scots Fusiliers, was mentioned in despatches, and won the Queen's and King's medals.

In 1906, transferred to the reserve, he put on another uniform – that of the peaked cap and leather cross-belt of the Corps of Commissionaires. He lived a quiet life in Glasgow, where, in 1908, he married Margaret Swift, who was a stenographer with the Corps. He was called up during World War I and wounded at Mons in 1914. After demobilisation, he joined (or returned to) the proud firm of Inglis, which was sold to the Harland and Wolff group in 1919 and continued to build ships until 1962. They built many steamers for the British India Steam Navigation Company and also a succession of Clyde steamers such as the famous paddle-steamer, the *Waverley*. Robert Willox held the responsible, if unskilled, post of gatekeeper, earning 50s. 3d. per week, supplemented, if you could so term it, by his war pension of 2s. 6d. For ten years Robert had lived next door at No 79 Grove Street to a fellow worker at the firm, named William Watts, but they were only on nodding terms, which was how, by choice, he conducted any relationships which were forced upon him.

On January 23rd 1929, Robert's wife, Margaret, died, but his temperamental oddity was already determined; bereavement was not the precipitating factor. The author understands that the novel *No Mean City* by Alexander McArthur and H Kingsley Long, published in 1935, was resented in Glasgow, seen as too violent and sensational, but it is, in fact, a moral tale with a deep layer of valuable social commentary. Set in the Gorbals, it seems, even so, to have application to Robert Willox's character: 'An understanding and reasoned contempt for one's neighbours, together with a fiercely unreasoning conviction of personal superiority, is not an uncommon phenomenon of the slum mind. Perhaps there is, all the time, a subconscious rebellion against conditions which are outwardly taken for granted. In face of all evidence to the contrary, he is still confident that the day will come when his superiority will compel recognition.'

In the matter of housing, 'It follows that society in the tenements is graded far more narrowly than in the outside world. One street may be definitely "better class" than another and not such good class as a third. Families that have two rooms look down upon those that live in a "single end".' The small Willox family, with both males in full employment, will have been regarded as highly respectable in their 'room-and-kitchen' apartment on the third floor or 'flat' with three other similar dwellings on the same level. All had been improved by the addition of an individual lavatory. That comfort aside, these were bleak times; there were no bathrooms, and there was only one cold-water tap in the kitchen sink. Sacks of coal were carried up the stairways by strong carters and stored in the lobbies or kitchen jawbox. The Willox family had a gas range and gas lighting. Water was heated on the range and there was a grate for a coal fire.

The kitchen could be kept warm, and there was nothing strange about the fact that Bertie and his father both slept in the kitchen, which measured 10 by 13 feet, one on a bedstead and the other probably in the typical bed-recess or 'cavity bed'. What does seem unusual is the state of the prized 'room' which was completely devoid of furniture. Another family would have let it, even if, like Robert Willox, they were admirably solvent. The furniture had not been pawned.

After the death of his wife, Robert took Bertie out of work to keep house for him, and paid him 2s. 6d. to 4s. 6d. a week, at the father's discretion. Outrageous as this seems to us – and Roughead considered the domestic conditions 'at once unnecessary and discomfortable' – it may have been a mere cultural expedient. The main breadwinner in an arduous job

(Robert left home at 4.45am for the Pointhouse Shipyard and returned at 6.00pm) expected someone resident in the apartment to prepare meals, buy in food, clean and wash. Gender was not always an important determinant. If the woman of the household was in employment and the man not so, the man would shop and cook. Robert did not, perhaps, intend Bertie's demotion to last forever and may have calculated that his own greater earning capacity was to be preserved at all costs. The Depression of 1930 was imminent, but, as it happened, A & J Inglis *did* survive.

Although Bertie accepted his new status with apparent resignation, inwardly a fierce resentment burned. He was generally regarded as a good boy. It was a miserable, reduced, existence for a 21-year-old lad who had recently lost his mother. There were many idle, aimless hours to fill and he used to wander round the streets with his friends, play billiards, and go to the cinema. His father was not good company. Dancing was all the rage, the dance-halls thronged, but he did not seek out girlfriends in any context.

There is a special edge to Roughead's commentary in a case where he had sat in court like a murderer's albatross in the seat specially reserved for his plumpish frame. Some there were (not Roughead) who saw Madeleine Smith plain. Roughead, who obviously rather liked, or felt much sympathy for, the fair-haired boy, managed to have a word with Bertie Willox at his appeal hearing, outside the court. It must have been an ordeal for Roughead, a most retiring person, to have pushed himself forward when he saw the opportunity, but a sense of duty will have impelled him. What he observed was interestingly to the point: 'a well-spoken, pleasant-mannered lad of rather effeminate type – most unsuitably cast, one should think, for the role of First Murderer.'

Bertie's drastically reduced circumstances left him short of the readies for cigarettes, his small amusements, and clothing, which was important to him. Roughead says that he 'had but two suits' – one was brown, the other black, yet, in fact, to have two 'whole suits' with waistcoats was an achievement in itself. He developed the habit of falsifying the household accounts to his own advantage, but was in continual fear of being found out. He was obviously afraid of Dada and the menace of the uniformed petty tyrant still perfuses the story of the crime.

It was a dark Monday, November 4th 1929, at 9.20 in the evening, and all was as quiet as it might be in that tall, gloomy building. In their three separate 'houses' on the third floor or flat, neighbours (Mrs G McKenzie, William Dale, and Mr and Mrs William Watt) were minding their own business. Then their ordinary lives suddenly moved into another dimension when young Bertie Willox, usually so well-behaved, began to bang on their respective doors and emit a kind of 'wailing howl'. They crowded on to the landing. The lad was extremely agitated and almost incoherent. 'Look! Look! Look!' was all they could make out.

He pointed to the open door of his apartment, which was illuminated by gaslight, and in its yellow glare they saw the body of Robert Willox in his commissionaire's uniform stretched in the lobby on the threshold of the kitchen, the head surrounded by a big blob of blood. No-one cared to enter in upon the lurid scene which lay within like an illustration from Thomas Burke's *Limehouse Nights*. There was of course no telephone available, and they sent Bertie off at a run to fetch the police. He arrived at the Northern Police Office at 9.30pm, in an exhausted condition and quite beside himself. 'Send an ambulance! Send an ambulance! My father is bleeding!' he informed the duty officer. Three times he 'swooned' and may genuinely have fainted. When they asked him what had happened, he made oblique answer that, 'My mother died some time ago'.

A pair of constables walked him back to Grove Street, and, on the way, he made the first of a series of discrepant, improvising remarks. There was no real guile in him, only horror and despair. He and his father, he said, had had their supper that evening, and he had then washed the dishes and set the table for breakfast before going out at 6.30pm. His father, he thought, must have fainted and cut his head against the iron bed. At the house, Robert Willox was obviously dead, with severe head injuries. The meal laid on the table in the kitchen spoke of supper, not breakfast, and supper prepared and not touched at that. A piece of boiled beef had been fished out, apparently in readiness for carving, from a pot of broth which rested on the range. Some vegetables from the broth lay on top of the beef. Crockery and cutlery were all clean. One report said that marmalade, sugar bowl, and teacups were all present, but that may not be accurate.

Inspectors called. The Yale lock on the front door was intact. Asked if there were a 'likely' weapon in the house, Bertie ingenuously mentioned a heavy coal hammer, and it was found in a kitchen cupboard, clean and dry, when it would have been expected to be covered in coal dust – unless Bertie were an exceptionally obsessional housekeeper. It was a 2lb engineer's hammer with a short wooden shaft and a double metal head.

Bertie's shoes, very wet, were found on the cross-bars below the table. He was now wearing boots, a waterproof, and a cap. It was a very rainy night, and the day could have been just as wet. The assumption was that the shoes, like the hammer, had been washed. His suit was discordant; he was wearing his black jacket and his brown trousers, but he could have been in the habit of mixing his clothes for variety of effect.

His neighbour, Mrs Watt, corroborated Bertie's account that Robert Willox had come home at 6.00pm. It appeared that he had been attacked very soon after entering the apartment, because he had not taken off his boots, and two daily papers, both unopened, and his spectacles, were still in the pockets of his overcoat, which was hanging up in the lobby. Only 2½d. was found on the corpse, and the lining of both trouser-pockets was bloodstained as if entered by an incarnadined hand. Blood had spattered all over the lobby and kitchen. The fire had gone out, but the grate was still warm. The sink looked clean. A damp towel hung from a nail, and a very wet dishcloth was folded up on the side of the sink.

A leaf torn from a scribbling-pad on the dresser bore confirmation of the ingredients of supper (and a general Monday replenishment): 'Monday. Bone, Vegetables, ¹/₄ stone potatoes, 1¹/₂ pints milk, ¹/₂ dozen eggs, 1lb. b.b. [boiling beef]'.

Professor Glaister, who held the chair of Forensic Medicine at Glasgow University, and Dr Campbell, casualty surgeon, arrived at midnight and examined the body and surroundings by the light of torches. At a subsequent post-mortem, the most important findings were that the hammer fitted the wounds, and that the stomach was entirely empty. No supper. There was no rigor mortis (but there had been a fire in the kitchen).

Bertie's several statements to the police were, in composite, that when he left home between 6.30 and 6.45pm, his father was sitting down polishing the buttons on his uniform tunic (which he was wearing when found). Bertie had had supper waiting for him – soup, rice-pudding, and a drink of milk, not tea, which he did not take in the evening, even on Sundays. There was no sign of rice-pudding, nor a glass of milk on the table, the lack of which would support his first story that, he Bertie, had washed up the supper things. If Dada had consumed only soup, not beef, that would nicely explain the uncut 'joint', even smaller after cooking, which, theoretically, could have been intended for a later occasion, and had been left out to cool. He could have taken only a little soup, because the pot was full up to 1¹/₄ inches from the top.

When his father came in that evening, he took off his coat and cap and himself hung them on the peg in the lobby. It was his habit to leave his keys dangling from his pocket-chain until he had hung up his coat, and then he put them in his pocket. (Significantly, however, the bunch of keys was found still attached to a trouser-button by a chain, lying on the floor behind the body – as if death had pre-empted the set routine.)

Bertie *did* *not* *know* who set the table as it was found (lame, this): probably it was his father, whose nightly custom it was to do so for the early breakfast next morning. (But he had already said that he, Bertie, had laid the table.)

Once out of the house and into the cooling rain, Bertie's movements round and about the neighbourhood were multiple and were well attested to by direct evidence. Accompanied by a 'pal', James Turner, aged 19, whom he had known since their schooldays, met by chance in Grove Street at, said Turner, 6.30pm, he played billiards at Sinclair's rooms at St George's Cross. Angus Duff, the manager, said that Bertie Willox played there nearly every night. (So Dada did not impose a curfew on Cinderella once duty had been done.) Bertie Willox and James Turner played there that night from 6.35 to 7.05pm and those precise times were marked out on the play sheet for Monday, November 4th. Bertie played under a strong light and was perfectly composed, with a steady hand and unwavering eye.

Further information which narrowed down the crucial times, lasting from 6.00pm until Bertie left the house, was provided by Isabella McKinney, who said that he was in the shop in Grove Street at which she worked, buying a packet of cigarettes at 6.25pm. Several other people encountered the two pals on their way to billiards. They tried, but did not succeed, to get free passes to the Empress Picture House, and Turner said that they had no money. He denied asking one Felix Carey to change him a pound, which Carey said that he saw – a green £1 note.

Moving on, Bertie had some debts to pay. He was still accompanied by Turner, who later denied it. Rain-drenched, he called on Mrs Margaret Duffy at No. 532 St George's Road, and gave her three £1 notes, a half-crown and one shilling. She gave him back sixpence for himself. The sum represented loans for shifty transactions such as redeeming a pledge on his father's war medals. Next, at about 7.15pm, he called on Denis Daly, of No. 91 Hopehill Road, salesman with the Household Supplies

Company, and squared an old account for £2. 14s. 11d., tendering and receiving change for a £5 note. He claimed that Dada had provided the cash that evening, specifying that Bertie was to pay the two creditors forthwith and 'get them off the map'. If the money was earmarked, then the two pals footloose in the street really did have no money to speak of. Bertie said that after paying the debts he was left with a few shillings for food shopping.

The wet, dismal evening was still not over, and at 7.30pm Bertie called at No. 490 St George's Road, where there lived a very good friend, Alfonso Jacovelli, who possessed the additional attraction of a real, working gramophone, which they played with for a time. Alfonso, aged 21, was married – Bertie had been his best man – and had known Bertie intimately for eight years. He knew all about Bertie's chronic impecuniosity since his mother's death, and his habit of pledging even Mother's rings, the aforesaid war medals, and the very bed sheets of the household. Sometimes he loaned him small sums.

It so happened that on the actual day of the murder, Alfonso had called on Cinderella at No. 79 Grove Street, between 1.00 and 2.00pm and, out of kindness, had invited him to spend the evening with him at St George's Road, to arrive at 7.30pm. Alfonso noticed that the Willox' table was set as for a meal. He was not an expected visitor, and this was no *mise-en-scène* for his benefit. There were two plates with a small piece of (unspecified) pudding on them, and some cold meat 'on the bunker' (the slab beside the sink). There was a pot on the gas range. Roughead wonders *en passant* why the table was 'thus spread and furnished between 1 and 2pm for a meal to be consumed at 6?' We can but surmise. The cold meat could have been Bertie's lunch. Roughead would not have known that boiling beef is notoriously tough and has to be simmered for hours. Most people prefer rice-pudding, hot, but it is not obligatory! A 'piece' does not sound like rice-pudding, but if stodgy enough it might qualify. A quantity might have been left over from Sunday. We cannot expect perfect culinary standards or timing from a boy of 20. He could well have made advance preparations on the principle of getting hated chores done. Two puddings would certainly indicate that Bertie was expecting to feed his father and was not premeditating an act which would deprive Dada of his pudding. It seems most unlikely that he was going to offer the pudding as a delicacy to another pal. Bertie complained to Alfonso that he was hard-up.

That evening at Alfonso's, Bertie said that he would not stay too long because he was tired and wanted to go to bed. (And tired he looks, in the *Weekly News* photograph taken the day after the murder.) 'He was quite cheery; some moments he was quiet' – as Alfonso had seen him often enough before. *He was wearing his brown trousers with his black jacket but between 1pm and 2pm he had been wearing his full brown suit.* Alfonso saw a small leather 'case' sticking out of Bertie's waistcoat pocket, and made a grab for it, just for fun, but was foiled. After a couple of hours, Alfonso accompanied his friend home as far as the corner of Grove and Scotia Streets, where they parted, said Alfonso, at 9.30pm. It was never seriously mooted that Bertie committed the murder and cleared up in the spare ten minutes before he alerted the neighbours, but, as if he wished to block any such potential suggestion, Bertie said that he looked into Meehan's shop before going home and spoke to Margaret Maguire (the assistant) who smiled but made no reply. She herself denied this incident. Up the stairs, then, he went, Bertie's statements concluded, to make the ghastly discovery.

A constable took him to an old friend, Mrs Smith, at No. 5 Canal Street, to spend the first night after the murder. The next day, Detective Inspector Stewart sat him down in the police office and asked him to show what money he had. Bertie produced 2s. 11d. He said that he absolutely did not know what money his father had had, because (a telling detail) he always doled it out to him in a secretive way, turning his back on his son. The Inspector then noticed – for yet again there was no attempt at concealment – a small leather wallet sticking out of the lad's waistcoat, which, on examination, revealed four £1 notes and four pawn-tickets. Bertie's explanation was that the £4 was payment from the *Weekly News* for an interview earlier that day, for a photograph of his father, and for allowing himself to be photographed (in preparation for which occasion he had gone to Thomas Duff, a barber, for a haircut, shampoo and shave). And, sure enough, J R M Christie, a staff reporter was able to confirm that he *had* paid over £3, not £4, and he actually identified those three notes found in the wallet. The spare £1 was suspiciously unaccounted for, and another small matter troubled the Inspector: Bertie was denying that he had paid Daly the debt owing with a £5 note even when Daly was brought to confront him. 'No,' said Bertie, 'I paid him three single pound notes.'

There were too many discrepancies and a dreadful deed seemed to dwell behind his candid, worried eyes. They arrested Bertie Willox and confiscated all his clothing for blood testing. The results were not strongly evidential of his guilt, considering that Professor Glaister counted 29 bloodstains upon the kitchen door alone. He found three small blood spots on the shirt worn presumably at the relevant time but he later admitted that they were probably 'exaggerated flea-bites'. On the brown jacket, brown waistcoat and brown trousers there were a few stains 'faintly positive of mammalian blood', and signs of washing by rubbing with a wet cloth. The wallet and all four £1 notes were completely free from bloodstains. The hammer, however, did show traces of mammalian blood. The damp towel and dish-cloth were not tested.

At the fiercely contested five-day trial begun on December 16th 1929, and held in the North Court, Glasgow, Bertie Willox did not give evidence on his own behalf, which was, no doubt, a wise decision, since he had already shown a tendency to weakness. A previously mooted plea of insanity had been abandoned after an examination by a team of alienists. A great deal of importance was attached to the evidence of Mrs Florence Watt, the next-door neighbour, supported by her husband, William, and a caller named Harrington (a witness later claimed by the defence). By unfortunate design, her lavatory was so positioned that it projected like a tongue into the kitchen and lobby area of the Willox' premises, in such a way that there were three partitioning walls, which provided the opportunity for embarrassing overhearing.

On the evening in question, Mrs Watt swore that, (although of course she could have been mistaken) at the vital time of 6.40pm 'or a little after half-past six', she let in William Harrington, who had called to see her husband. Harrington said the time was about 6.37pm. She then went into the lavatory for a couple of minutes and while she was thus engaged, she swore that she heard an altercation between Robert and Bertie Willox. It was not the first time; there had been similar trouble on the preceding Friday and Saturday. 'You won't get a penny from me!' she heard the father say. He was 'going for' the boy. For the Crown, this was strong evidence of imminent violence, but for the dogged defence, this was equally strong evidence that there had been a dispute with another person, far too late for Bertie to be present, proved, as he was, to have been at the billiards rooms at 6.35pm. It must be said that the Court of Criminal Appeal was to be sympathetic to the latter view, but not that sympathetic...

It transpired that Alfonso had not been Bertie's only visitor. An agent, Henry Cox, called at one o'clock for a life insurance premium but was fobbed off: Bertie said that his father would be out at the doctor's that night. Nor had Bertie stayed in all day; for quite apart from the heavy load of food shopping, he had also, between 1.00 and 2.00pm, tried to pledge those shoes later found very wet under the table, with Alexander McLeod, a pawnbroker, who declined them, as too worn. On the timing of the attack, Hector Kennedy, a canvasser for the municipal elections failed to get a reply at the Willox' apartment at 8.30pm On a nasty point for the Crown, the shop assistant, Isabella McKinney said that, the morning after the crime, Bertie had told her that he had been through a 'terrible ordeal' and that he had made 'one slip'.

The jury convicted by a majority of nine to six. Roughhead would have preferred Not Proven. The Appeal Court thought that Not Proven would not have been unreasonable, but, even so, would not overturn the verdict. The capital sentence was commuted to penal servitude for life, which, come to think of it, was merely a continuation of the life of drudgery in the tenement in Glasgow.

William Bennison was a cross between Dr Pritchard of Glasgow and George Joseph Smith, an eliminator of unwanted wives and set fair to multiply into a mass murderer. He was also a bigamist, which goes with that type of criminality. In 1850, when he was caught, the Victorian mind was most interested in his vile hypocrisy. Today, we are more engaged by the hypocritical politician, but at that time the contrast between his domestic cruelty and his canting, ranting religious enthusiasm was thought to be edifying to contemplate.

The soil from which he sprang fully armed with a name fit, save for the double consonant, for the profession of his faith, was Irish. His background was poor, and he could not even write his own name. All the family, according to his sister, Mary Bennison, were baptised into the Church of England persuasion and perhaps she meant the United Church of England and Ireland. In his youth – and he was aged 32 in 1850 – he had eagerly embraced Primitive Methodism, the movement founded in 1805 by William Clowes of Burslem and Hugh Bourne of Stoke-on-Trent, and so named in 1812. They had been expelled from the Wesleyan Church for persisting in holding open-air revival meetings with singing and exhortations.

Bennison could not read the Gospels but he was fluent and rhetorical in prayer and able to inspire others, described as a great proselytiser, a shining light, and an assiduous visitor of the sick. There has been a misapprehension that he was a preacher, but he obviously could not be an ordained minister, nor a lay or 'local preacher' of whom standards were demanded. He attended the 'class-meetings' regularly and was regarded as a pillar of the chapel. There was no insanity in him. He was no religious monomaniac, a favourite cultural figure of the 19th century. His religious zeal did not rule the other compartments of his life, and he was not irrational. Certainly he showed the symptoms of lack of moral conscience in himself, cold egoism, lack of empathy with others (to the ultimate degree!) but that is another matter.

In person he was the embodiment of the preacher man, of forbidding hawkish aspect, able even so to thrill the ladies, and endowed with a persuasive Irish accent. On November 5th, 1838, at Tavanagh, near Portadown, in Armagh, he married a girl named Mary Mullen. After little more than a year, he deserted her and left Ireland, settling in Paisley, where on December 5th, 1839, he bigamously took part in a marriage ceremony with a delicate girl named Jane Hamilton. There is no evidence that financial gain was a part of his motivation in changing from Mary to Jane. He was born to poverty and lived all his brief life in poor circumstances, except for being in receipt of a small windfall just before the end. He had no known occupation or income at all. Wearying of Jane after only a few weeks, he returned to Mary in Ireland and persuaded her to go back to Scotland with him. She went unwillingly, because he had beaten her. Poor young Mary was a Methodist, and when she sailed away with him, she was wearing a blue mantle. Once in Scotland, in Airdrie, she was never seen again by her family and it was later thought by people in responsible positions that he had soon murdered her.

Jane Hamilton had been advised by a friend, Margaret Ross, of Bathgate, not to marry William Bennison. She took him back after his unexplained absence in Ireland, having lived in the interim with her sister, Helen. The returned voyager was dressed ominously in mourning clothes, with a crêpe band on his hat. He said, ridiculously, that his sister had travelled with him, had suffered from seasickness on the passage, and had subsequently died at Airdrie. Under his arm was a bundle of what he said were his sister's clothes, which he gave, by way of peace offering to Jane. The blue mantle was well received. Afterwards, it was inevitable that Jane should find out that his sister was still alive, and she taxed him with the monstrous lie. He joked, and passed it off, saying that she was 'only a Sister in the Lord'.

The bigamous marriage survived for some ten years and a daughter was born in about 1843. From Paisley, they had moved to Edinburgh, where they occupied an apartment in Stead's Place, off Leith Walk. In a modern phrase, they occupied separate rooms, because of Jane's poor health. She had a cough, and ailed in the winter. Also a Methodist, it appears, she was gentle and pious and devoted to her child. Bennison was becoming tired of her and his fierce eye alighted on Margaret Robertson, his favourite convert, who began to share his pew in the Methodist chapel at Leith under the benign gaze of the Reverend Mr John Hay. Jane languished indoors while this was going on, and begged her husband to stay at home and 'make family worship', but he replied that he needed outdoor exercise and did not have enough time for family worship as well as attendance at prayer-meetings. Her sister, Helen, thought it better not to tell her that she had often seen William and Margaret Robertson out walking in the evenings. Helen was conscious that Jane was 'low-spirited' when alone, although she put up a brave front in company. For her constitutional weakness, she took only one medicine – cream of tartar, which she kept on an open shelf in the kitchen cupboard. This old remedy would have been no earthly use in the amelioration of her 'bad chest', being a mere purgative and diuretic. (The substance, incidentally, occurs in the later stages of the fermentation of grape-juice, found deposited on the sides of the cask, and is known as 'argol'. Dissolved in hot water, the solution is filtered and the pure cream of tartar crystallised out. It is *not* the poison known as tartar emetic or tartarated antimony.)

Mary Robertson, who lived at McNeill's Place, Leith Walk, with her mother and sister, the Margaret Robertson who shared the Bennison pew, was to say that when the good man visited their house, 'the conversation was always of religion'. Margaret was a serious girl, she said, incapable of wrong, and when they walked together in the evenings, they were simply going home from meetings. Bennison, however, was not content with their relationship as it stood, and he began to make preparations. Six weeks before Jane Bennison died, he went to a chemist's shop, owned by William Macdonald, and was served by the wife, Jane Macdonald. He was well known to both of them. He told her that he wanted to buy some arsenic for rats. She asked him to wait until her husband came in, but he said that there was no use waiting; he was in a hurry because his wife was too nervous to go for the coals, being so frightened of the myriads of rats which infested the cellar. Respectful of the good man and aware of his poverty, Mrs Macdonald obliged him, and gave good value for his twopence – between half and three-quarters of an ounce.

Twopence appears by repetition of account to have been the sum regularly proffered in Victorian times for 'arsenic for rats' but it is interesting that the quantity or the quality (i.e. the extent of the adulteration by other substances) supplied should have varied according to the chemist's knowledge of the purchaser.

In anticipation, Bennison joined two funeral societies and paid to the agent, Andrew Carr, in all, the sum of 1s. 5d. He also joined a benefit society, the terms of which were that he would get £3 in respect of the loss of his wife, and that the members were each to give him one shilling to provide a coffin, in the event of such a sad necessity. Jane now had one week to live, and he told her sister, who was surprised, that Jane was 'breaking up'.

On Friday evening, April 12th, in that frugal household, Jane ate a little porridge for supper and was taken with violent pain and sickness. Bennison lay low right through Saturday and then on the Sunday sprang into activity. Off to sister Helen to tell her to come at once if she wanted to see Jane alive; the doctor said she would slip away in a few hours. As he spoke, he seemed upset, and asked for a glass of spirits. Dr Gillespie had indeed had a look at the sick woman but had not made the reported comment, nor had he been called in as a matter of urgency: he had happened to be passing along Stead's Place, and Bennison had asked him to come in and see his wife. He found the patient very weak, gave directions for treatment, and told the husband to send word to the dispensary if she became worse. He heard no more.

Out to the chemist Bennison scurried, to William Macdonald of course, where he was known and trusted. All night, he said, his poor Jane had been ill. The chemist dispensed two powders, containing cinnamon, ginger and cayenne pepper, all of which were used indeed (on checking) in gastric ailments, but all of course powerless against the stronger agent which the same shop had provided.

Helen sat with her clearly dying sister and gave her some wine and milk with water, and gruel, but naturally she could keep nothing down. Bennison wandered in and out and Helen thought his manner very cool. He asked for 'the dead-clothes' to be looked out and enquired about the correct form of funeral letters. He never spoke to his wife. There were other witnesses of the frightful scene. A neighbour, Mrs Porteous, of Stead's Place, was greatly surprised when Bennison appeared at her door and said that his wife was very ill and that 'he doubted her very much in that bout'. Jane had been in her usual health when she had seen her just the other day. She offered to fetch a doctor but he said that he had a low opinion of doctors and knew better what medicine to give her. She went round, and found Jane vomiting into a tub. She did not like Bennison's manner; it was strange and not right. She asked him to send for a doctor, as this was obviously not Jane's usual chest trouble, but he refused. When he tried to give his wife a drink, he did not look her in the eye, but stood at the crown of her head and reached forward to her mouth – a most unnatural action.

John Porteous was also there and Bennison told him that he had tried to contact four doctors, but they were all engaged. Euphemia Ingram, a niece of clever Mrs Porteous, also saw Mrs Bennison vomiting in the tub. She saw some discarded porridge and potatoes and offered to give them to the Bennisons' pig, but of course he did not want his valuable commodity to be poisoned and answered hastily that it would be a waste of 'good meat', and that he would give the food to 'Sandy's dog'. Agnes Turnbull, hearing of Mrs Bennison's illness, went to see her on Sunday, after chapel, and, appalled, she too, offered to run for a doctor, but Bennison said it was no use, 'She was going home; she was going to glory'.

During the night of the Sunday, Jane cried out, begging for a doctor but, in her hearing, Bennison said that there was no use incurring further expense; the doctor had done everything possible, and she could not put off many hours. Besides, he said, the doctor was coming again in the morning. No doctor came. There had been only the one consultation. The minister had been to the house. He said that he had received a note from Bennison asking for the congregation to pray for his wife. (Since he could not write we must presume that one of the neighbours helped him.) The Reverend John Hay found Mrs Bennison very ill but noticed nothing untoward.

After a severe struggle, Jane Bennison died on Monday, April 15th, at midday, comforted by her sister, and friends. Bennison was out at the time. Elizabeth Grindlay, a neighbour who was present at the death, met Bennison at the door when he came back and told him. 'Thank God! She has gone to glory. She has gone home', he intoned. He told the sister that he had met the doctor at the door and told him that he need not go up, as it was all over. The funeral, he declared, was to take place on Wednesday: there was no use (his favourite, pragmatic phrase) wasting time. This is exactly the tone of George Joseph Smith's elegiac words on his wives – 'When they're dead, they're dead'. Sandy's dog died. It belonged, in fact, to Alexander Milne who lived on the same floor in the building as the Bennisons. The good man had come to him, bearing a bowl of cold potatoes for his dog, thinking of him even when his wife so ill. That was on the Sunday. The dog finished the bowl at 2.00pm and it began to moan at 7.30pm. He found it lifeless the next morning. It may have been that Bennison was of the numerous tribe of dog-haters, or he may have had it in for Sandy's dog in particular, but the motivation is more likely to have been sheer cunning. Surrounded by anxious neighbours, and under observation, he knew that throwing away good food would have been construed as strange behaviour.

Now, at last, Bennison was able to import Margaret Robertson into his humble abode, and he watched with secret rejoicing as she made tea with Jane's crocks on the very day of the death. She was to visit him daily from then on and the neighbours saw that he showed no signs of grief for his loss. This was careless of him, but he was in a stage of high elation. The minister was surprised when he asked for the early funeral on the Wednesday, thinking it too soon and against propriety, but Bennison won the day with a characteristic axiom – it did not do for poor people to keep a corpse long in the house. Margaret delivered the funeral invitations by hand. Bennison collected from the various societies, and told a William Fairgrieve that he stood to gain £11 all told. He also collected from Mrs Ramsay the pair of black trousers which he had asked her to mend for him when, he said, his wife was lying poorly, and if there were a change, he would need to make himself decent. This time, he made the ill-judged remark that he had seen many a deathbed, but never a pleasanter one than his wife's. As it happened, Mrs Ramsay had noticed him going about with Miss Robertson for a couple of months before Jane died. He told William Fairgrieve that when she was taken ill, his wife begged him to marry again, because he would be poorly treated in lodgings.

The friends and neighbours and sister Helen were stunned by the shock of the sudden death and Bennison's nonchalance. Elizabeth Wilkie, who lived below the Bennisons, on the area floor, was exhausted because the noise of poor Jane's retching had kept her awake all night. Bennison was invited to spend his first night without Jane at the Robertsons'. Helen felt that there was definitely something wrong, and on the Wednesday morning bravely confronted Bennison and told him that she wanted a post-mortem. He refused saying that his feelings could never stand the strain, and Jane had died happy, what more could Helen want? Not convinced, she stood her ground, and he said that he would fetch Dr Gillespie to satisfy her, but after an absence of half an hour, he returned alone, claiming that the doctor had gone to the country. The funeral took place on the Wednesday as planned and Jane Bennison was buried in Rosebank Cemetery, Pilrig Street. A copy of her burial record is shown as an appendix to the *Scots Black Kalendar*, (first published in Perth in 1938): Jane Bennison's age is given as 40, and the disease stated is consumption.

When the shameful funeral was over, Helen, with the support of Jane's friend, Mrs Moffat, went to lay information with the procurator fiscal. On the Thursday, Bennison oiled his way back to the chemist, William Macdonald and asked for a 'line' to prove the two powders which he had previously bought, explaining that his neighbours were raising suspicions about his wife's death. The chemist said that it was not necessary. Then, said Bennison carefully, 'What about THAT I got from you? Will they harm me about it?' The chemist asked what he meant, and he said 'THAT thing, the arsenic.' He had simply given it to his wife to use, and had never seen it again.

As, he went on, no-one else knew about the purchase of the poison, he would deem it a great favour if the chemist did not mention it. Further, he wheedled, since it was actually Mrs Macdonald who gave him the arsenic, he could truthfully say that he did not provide it. Unimpressed by this casuistry,

Macdonald suggested shortly that Bennison should tell the authorities himself. He did question him as to the course of the illness, and observed that it was 'singular' but he was not suspicious always thinking that this was a Christian and a man of undoubted piety. 'Could they bring me up for it if arsenic were found in the body?' Bennison asked. The chemist thought they could. 'Ah well', said Bennison, 'God has carried me through many difficulties and will do so now, I am sure.'

The exhumation took place very soon, on the Friday. Helen identified the body and she heard Bennison say that 'he would not for ten pounds' have had it raised. At some time, she went to Bennison and asked him where the rat poison was kept, and he said that it had been used; he had handed it over to Jane and then gone out to a meeting. The Macdonalds must have talked, because before then, Helen had never heard of rats in the house, or of poison being used. Nor had the neighbours, now that the truth was out, nor Mrs Porteous, nor sleepless Elizabeth Wilkie, whose coal cellar was situated immediately below Bennison's and who had never seen a whisker in twelve years' residence, even though she kept fowls in the area (next to Bennison's store-pig [sic], presumably).

Sheriff officer George Ferguson was present at the exhumation, observing the suspect, William Bennison, as he identified the body as his 'dear Jane'. Later that day, he proceeded to Stead's Place where he found Bennison cowering in the illusory sanctuary of his own bed. He arrested him and removed him into custody, together with a small tub and a pot. In the press in the kitchen he found some powders, which were probably the chemist's harmless remedies, untouched. In the cellar, however, he found in the 'dross' a piece of paper which did contain particles of arsenic. There was no sign of rat infestation.

The post-mortem showed no symptoms in any of the organs of recent acute disease, although the deceased had formerly suffered from 'inflammation of the lungs' and had been subject to asthma. Upon chemical analysis, sufficient arsenic (the quantity not stated) to cause death was traced in a gritty substance taken from the stomach, in the tissue of the stomach, and in the liver. The iron porridge pot seemed to have been carefully cleaned and there was no arsenic detected in it. Minute traces, however, were found in the tub. The piece of whitey-brown paper had been used for wrapping up arsenic. The doctors, on the same occasion, examined the body of Sandy's dog, but found no evidence of arsenic. They did comment that dogs vomit with greater facility than human beings and are more efficient at eliminating poison. Another dead dog, belonging to a Mr Waldie, was also tested for arsenic, with negative results.

The trial of William Bennison for murder and bigamy began on July 25th 1850, at the High Court of Justiciary, Edinburgh. It was noticed that the accused looked 'haggard and careworn' but there was still enough power in his gaze for Mrs Porteous to falter in her evidence, whereupon the judge reprimanded him for the attempt to intimidate. He had emitted several loathsome declarations, and these were read in court at the close of the evidence for the prosecution, which had been strong and detailed. His statement was that on the Saturday he had set forth in quest of medical aid for his wife's sudden illness but could not find a doctor. He wanted to try again in the afternoon, but his wife would not let him. He had told her to be careful with the rat poison. He denied his first true marriage, but later admitted the marriage to Mary Mullen. He had not actually deserted her: it was her suggestion that he should try Scotland since he could not get work in Ireland. Six months later, he heard that she was dead, and he believed himself to be a widower when he married Jane Hamilton. He was most surprised, when visiting his parents in Ireland, to learn that Mary was, in fact, still alive. He lived with her for two nights and they then left Belfast for Glasgow. The passage was very stormy and she suffered much. They went by coach to Airdrie, where she was taken ill and died in three days. Two doctors attended her. Because of the unfortunate mistake over the two marriages, he put no name on the coffin and was the only mourner at the funeral. What else could he do then but return to his dear Jane with the white lie about the death of his sister? Afterwards he did confess the circumstances of his first marriage to her and she begged him never to tell her sister, Helen.

The star witness for the defence was Margaret Robertson, who was defending her own reputation as much as Bennison's life. She stated that she had a leaning to Methodism long before March, when she met Mr Bennison. None of her family was a Methodist, and they disapproved of her going to meetings. She knew that he was a married man and she never regarded him as a sweetheart. 'I declare upon my oath that there was no courtship between us.' He visited her home to offer up a prayer for her mother, who was poorly. She herself, she admitted, had thought that he 'came too much about her' but she lacked the courage to tell him so. Her own mother spoke to her about it when Mrs Bennison was alive.

One witness was there to attest to rats in Stead's Place. Alexander Murray, who lived 19 yards from the Bennisons' home, gave evidence to the effect that his premises were overrun with rats. He had caught eleven in his coal-bunker and had seen one a few days ago. A valiant attempt was made to refute the charge of bigamy; James Gibson, an Irish barrister, had stated for the Crown that a marriage celebrated by a dissenting clergyman between two dissenters, without proclamation of banns, would, in 1838, have been a good and valid marriage as the law stood. The defence tried to show that the first marriage was invalid, because Bennison was a baptised member of the Church of England, but the judge indicated to the jury that the prisoner had failed to prove that fact.

After 20 minutes' deliberation, the jury returned verdicts of guilty of murder and bigamy. Bennison reacted with his usual pragmatism, remarking to the officer beside him in a matter-of-fact way, as if he were a mere observer, 'It is of *both* the charges'. The Lord Justice-Clerk before formally pronouncing the death sentence, deliberately cast off the obligation to say something of improving import, because of the peculiar nature of the case. He addressed the prisoner: 'When we find that you had professions of sanctity in your mouth even at the time that your unhappy wife was dying before your eyes as the result of poison administered to her by you, I feel it were vain to hope that anything I could say would have any effect upon your mind.'

William Bennison, very composed, then fully ratified that elegant and measured summation of his mentality as his strong Irish tones rang out in the shocked courtroom: 'I do not blame the Court or the jury for their verdict but I say that I can here solemnly declare before God that I am innocent. I do solemnly before God pray earnestly for those that came up yesterday against me. I do solemnly forgive them this day.'

The Reverend Mr Hay, feeling the awkwardness of his wrong opinion of the man, was, however a match for Bennison and wrought upon him unremittingly until a confession was obtained, and sent to the Home Office. It was leaked to the *Courant* for all to savour:

His child having previously gone to bed, and Bennison having on the score of illness excused himself from eating anything that night, his wife was the only one that partook of the porridge, and to that her death is to be ascribed. He states that the girl Robertson had not the most remote idea that he had any interest in her except that of a religious kind [which would appear to be a confession of the nature of his interest in her] and that he never spoke to her unless in respect to her spiritual welfare.

The *Courant* hoped that there might be a confession of murder of the first wife – arsenic was strongly suspected – but Bennison drew back from that. No later writer seems to have searched for a record of that coffin without a name lost in a graveyard in Airdrie. On August 16th, William Bennison was publicly despatched by hoary old Murdoch of Glasgow, and a minor Oscar Wilde described the occasion in a street-ballad:

> They led him out all clad in black –
> Black coat and vest so white –
> A mocking smile was on his lips,
> He wore a nosegay bright.

'Holy Willie' they called him, with perhaps a touch of Shakespearean bawdy, and on the edge of death he 'joined in the devotions with apparent fervour and at intervals uttered a deep response, his face wearing almost an habitual smile'. He left the world after a severe struggle.

CHAPTER 10
A TRYST WITH DR SMITH

To appreciate the perfidy of Dr William Smith (for the modern mind revolts against the jury verdict of Not Proven) we must first envisage the trusted family doctor, sole practitioner in a remote rural community in the 1850s, struggling with dire matters of life and death, attending frightening home confinements, facing up to 'lunatics' stricken with 'mania', preparing tinctures and potions, and driving out in all weathers to isolated farmsteads. A married man, he was London qualified, but had chosen to live and work in a far corner of Aberdeenshire, in the old village of St Fergus, lying back behind the coastline, five miles to the north-west of Peterhead. Perhaps a farmer *manqué*, he had bought up three fields around the village, in which he will have grazed stock for profit. His 'offices' or surgery were in the demesne of his house in the village, where he kept a pig and interested himself in the garden. He grew dahlias. Two servants, Martha Cadger and Eliza Park, made up the modest establishment. There was no affluence.

For some reason, in 1852, perhaps desiring to increase his agricultural holdings, or even (and this is pure speculation) to redress some gambling debts, he conceived the urgent need to lay his hands on a substantial sum of money. The perfect murder demands proactive measures, especially if an insurance fraud is contemplated. For a full seven years the doctor had looked after the medical needs of the McDonald family – widowed mother, daughter Agnes, and three sons, Charles, Robert and William – farming at Burnside, about two miles out from the village.

William, the eldest, aged 29, was the son that Dr Smith was interested in. Although so young, he was a widower, engaged to marry again, to a girl named Mary Slessor who lived at Hill of Mintlaw, some seven miles distant. They planned to marry as soon as he could find a suitable farm to rent, and had saved up enough funds from the wages paid to him by his mother. Sobered, no doubt, by his early experience of loss, he was thought of as hard-working, kind, and a great reader of the Bible. In spite of the difference in social class, a friendship had developed between the doctor and the young farmer. Let us hope that the liking had grown before the doctor's plan had taken shape. It is difficult to imagine what they found to talk about, other than the land and animal husbandry. Latterly, William had been consulting the doctor as to likely farms. Dr Smith was his oracle and mentor, and he was completely under his influence. There are hints that his mother was not entirely happy about the unusual friendship. There is no strong indication that it was an *amitié particulière*.

A new element was beginning to creep into their conversation – the topic of life insurance. William understood none of it, but if Dr Smith told him to, he would sign anything. Dr Smith approached three separate insurance companies – the Scottish Union, the Northern, and the Caledonian – and insured the life of his young friend, William McDonald for the total sum of £2,000, in favour of the proposer, Dr William Smith. A person may only insure a life in which he can show that he has a pecuniary interest. For example, he may insure against the death of someone who owes him money. You cannot insure the life of anyone who takes your fancy.

James Hutchinson, agent for the Northern Insurance Company, scenting a rat, made further enquiries of Dr Smith, but he proved a wily fox and apparently satisfied Hutchinson by explaining that he had an insurable interest which was dependent on the life of a third party from whom he expected double the amount proposed to be insured. The real meaning of this mysterious mumbo-jumbo lay in the story that one William Milne, William McDonald's uncle, owed the doctor £46 for professional attendance. William was expecting to succeed to his uncle's farm. There is logic to it, and for good measure, the doctor sent up his fit, healthy body, William McDonald, to satisfy the insurers' medical examiners at Peterhead. There was more to it, though: the general rule is that a policy fails if the life insured ends by suicide, but in this case the doctor saw to it that a special clause was written in to vitiate that possibility. It must be quite clear by now that Dr Smith intended to see to it that his protégé would become a *felo-de-se*. Meanwhile, Uncle William died but did not leave his farm to William McDonald. The policies stood and William's disappointment could be grist to the doctor's mill as a trigger to suicide. All oblivious, William continued to lean on his wise friend. 'The Doctor's a fine chiel, and I have always done as he bade me,' he had told the insurance agents.

The dark day came on Saturday November 19th, 1853. From dawn to eve, William laboured on the farm, his head full of plans. In a few days' time he was going to see his Mary Slessor at Mintlaw market, and on the following Tuesday he was going to see his brother, Charles, who had just left home to work on a neighbouring farm, Langside. That Saturday evening, he had an immediate appointment or 'tryst' with Dr Smith at his stable door in the village, and had to be there at 6 o'clock. He set off in the 'gloaming', on foot, before 5 o'clock and the tryst may be presumed to have taken place, because by 7 o'clock we can place him, perfectly happy, in the still open and lighted shop of James Smith, the village cartwright. Here he ordered some hames to be made (those being the two curved bars of a draught-horse's collar), and also a grub-harrow for turnips. He said he would be needing some palings for the farm. For half an hour he stayed talking to some friends, in excellent spirits, before saying that it was getting late and he needed to be away home. It was just before 7.30pm when he left the shop.

That night, he did not come home, and on the Sunday morning, his brother Robert went out to look for him. The nearest way down to the village was by a path leading through Dr Smith's six-acre field to a road which went toward the doctor's stable. There was a break in the hedge which crossed the field, and in this sheltered place Robert found his brother lying dead in a ditch. There was what looked like a bullet wound in the right cheek, and the face was pitifully blackened with gunpowder. The body lay on its back in about one inch of water, and he pulled the head up on to the bank. When he did this, he found a pistol beside the ditch, four feet distant from the head in its original position. Robert McDonald ran to fetch the doctor, but he was out, so he left a message and returned to the ditch. He stood there, crying. Soon he saw Dr Smith and James Pirie, the village farrier, coming up from the main road. Dr Smith stood over the body. He seemed horrified. 'God preserve us!' he exclaimed, holding his hands to the sky. He picked up the pistol: 'That's the thing that's done it.' All three of them drew the body out of the ditch. The doctor said that William was 'partly shot and partly drowned'. The wound was caused by a wad (the packing used to keep the charge in the gun), not by a bullet – that was his opinion, and it was a clear case of suicide. No-one (except the jury) ever accepted that opinion.

They carried the body to the nearest house, that of James Fordyce, where a preliminary search of the clothing was made. There was neither powder nor shot in his pockets, only a watch and snuffbox. William never carried money. He was wearing a kind of 'polka' (a tight-fitting jacket, often knitted, generally given as a woman's garment) the pockets of which were too small to hold the pistol. A small point, but relevant. The body was trundled off home to Burnside by cart, and Dr Smith made for the farm on foot to break the news to Mrs McDonald. On the way, he met Mr Alexander Moir, Minister of the Free Church and informed him that William had shot himself. Bereaved Mrs McDonald would not accept it. Her son had never had a pistol.

There had been no family quarrels (for the doctor kept trying to insinuate that idea) and her son did not have a pistol. She must have been suspicious when she asked Dr Smith if he had met her son, as arranged, at the stable door at 6 o'clock, and he denied that there had been any such arrangement.

Dr William Smith, friend of the family, certified the death:

> *St Fergus, 20th November, 1853*
>
> *I do hereby certify, on soul and conscience, that I was called upon this morning about half-past nine o'clock, by Robert McDonald, to see his brother William, who was found in a field near St Fergus and who had received a shot from a pistol in the right cheek, taking an upward and backward direction. There was a small quantity of blood coming from the ear and nostrils, the face completely covered with powder, so that the pistol must have been close to him, and from the direction it takes, I infer that it is not likely to have been done by any other than the deceased.*
>
> *W Smith, M.R.C.S.L.*

He took over all the funeral arrangements, pressing first for Tuesday, which was changed to Wednesday by forces outside his control. Rashly, he observed to the mother that if Boyd heard what had happened, he would soon be out. Boyd was the procurator fiscal, well known to the other professional man, and, sure enough he did arrive from Peterhead on the Monday morning. A post-mortem and an examination of the locus were carried out on that same day.

Dr Comrie, who practised in Peterhead, and Dr Gordon, a retired naval surgeon from New St Fergus, inspected the ditch and found that it was 18 inches deep with longish grass and decayed matter at the bottom, under about an inch of stagnant water. The impression of the body showed up clearly. The surrounding ground was hard and dry with no sign of any struggle. On the west bank, there was a mark of blood, which was incomprehensible if the deceased had stood in the ditch and shot himself. He had not suffocated or drowned. Death was instantaneous and the pistol must have been fired only a few inches from the head – say three to twelve. If shot by another, that person would have had to be at his side. On tracing the course of the wound to the cheek, the doctors found a pistol bullet lodged in one of the convolutions in the middle lobe of the left hemisphere of the brain. If the man had shot himself, he must have been sitting in the ditch. If he fell outside the ditch, it would have been a matter of a few seconds for another person to put the body into the ditch. An accident was inconceivable. (This had been one theory which Dr Smith had put about.)

Neither doctor would commit himself on the option between suicide or murder, except that Dr Gordon, who had actually known William McDonald, was in a position to give his professional opinion that he was not of suicidal disposition. He also shrewdly commented that, after making some experiments, he would have expected a suicide to have held the pistol closer to the head, and he thought it remarkable that the pistol had been aimed a little above the gums, whereas a suicide traditionally aimed at the ear or temple.

That Monday evening, feeling a chill wind of insecurity, Dr Smith repaired to the manse, where he told the minister that he was 'disappointed' with 'that McDonald widow' because she had been saying that her son had been murdered. Mr Moir observed that it seemed to him that there was a good deal of mystery about the tragedy, which ought to be looked into. He faced Dr Smith and asked him bluntly, 'Where were you on Saturday night?' The doctor reeled off a series of calls and events. If some stranger had done the deed, said the minister, it was curious that the body had been found so easily, as it was a path seldom used by anyone except the McDonalds, the doctor, and the minister. He asked Dr Smith how it was that he found the body, and he said that he had heard the brother's lamentations.

On Tuesday, November 22nd, Dr Smith spoke to a friend, James Greig, a local farmer, who told him that the Fiscal had been asking about insurance policies. The doctor had been inclined to deny all association with the insurances, but he now admitted to Greig that he expected to get £1,500 or £1,000 from them. Well then, said his friend, only joking, 'They'll blame you for pistolling McDonald!' And so they did, for they came for the doctor that very day and arrested him for murder. Detained at Peterhead awaiting trial, he made three inconsistent and lying declarations. He swore that there was no tryst. He himself had not effected any insurances. The late William Milne had done it for his (the doctor's) benefit. Milne gave him the money for it. He was not even sure if he had the policies. There were three of them, he believed, and he did not know the conditions. He certainly did not know that he stood to benefit on the death of William McDonald. Anyway, he did not expect the sums to be paid out, because it was a case of suicide. He was convinced that it was suicide.

Whose pistol was it? (The bullet found in the brain fitted the pistol, incidentally.) Not William's, said the family. Not mine, said the doctor, cheerfully owning up to one broken pistol discovered at his home by the police. However, enquiries revealed that at the end of August that year he had bought a *second* pistol from a shop in Peterhead, paying 4s. 6d. for it. He had also bought two dozen percussion-caps. Confronted with the pistol which had killed William McDonald, the shop assistant could not swear that it was the one which he had sold to Dr Smith, whom he knew. He could only say that it was of the same class and of similar make. This was, of course, extremely lucky for the doctor, but, even so, he was unable to account for a second pistol which had come into his possession and his defence lawyers were to make no attempt to show what had become of it. This point speaks for itself.

Gunpowder was found at Dr Smith's house, but he quickly accounted for it by saying that he required it for use in an ointment for a patient named Margaret Reid. It was by way of a repeat prescription. He had not opened the new packet. Gunpowder is composed of charcoal, saltpetre and sulphur. It must, presumably, have been in clinical use, because Dr Smith could otherwise have expected the derision and disbelief of his peers. Sulphur, certainly, was widely used for skin complaints, but it was immediately obtainable in non-explosive compound. It is difficult to justify the need for the other two components. (The treatment of haemorrhoids, perhaps!) Anyway, the previously dispensed pot of ointment, on retrieval from Margaret Reid, contained no gunpowder at all, no doubt to her relief. The packet of gunpowder had in fact been opened, and the string of it cut. The contents weighed only one and three quarter ounces, whereas two ounces had been sold to him. Dr Smith was well equal to this difficulty; the procurator fiscal must have burst the packet during his brutal search of the premises. Indeed the fiscal did confess that a small quantity, 'not half a teaspoonful', had been spilt at the time, but the fiscal 'made a pinch of it, and put it back'. Joseph Harkom, gunmaker of Edinburgh, deposed that it would not take more than the eighth part of a quarter of an ounce of gunpowder to fire the ball in question from the pistol found, but this was not entirely against Dr Smith who could say that the large quantity acquired by him demonstrated its medicinal use.

However, the actual process of acquisition of the packet proved to be an embarrassment to the doctor, because it evidenced a furtiveness and an urgency quite out of keeping with an innocent use. On the day *before* the death, he had gone over to New St Fergus and tried, without success, to buy some gunpowder for the purpose of shooting crows. In the end, he had bought the two ounces of the stuff from McLeod's shop in his own village, 'a little before dark' on the exact day of the death, the Saturday evening when the shutters were still down and people lingered in the shops in the relaxed time before the Sabbath.

Alibi was the corner-stone of Dr Smith's defence, and he had laid a winding trail, deliberately studded with clues as to time. Time was of the essence, because the distance from the doctor's house to the ditch in his field was only 500 yards, which, according to a land surveyor, could easily be walked in three minutes and forty-five seconds. The time of the pistol-shot was put by several witnesses at 7.35 or 7.36pm on the Saturday evening, the specificity easily achieved by the fact that the death had occurred so close to the village that the shot had been heard and the flash seen.

It will be remembered that William McDonald left the cartwright's shop at 7.30pm. According to Dr Smith, he himself had been at home from 7.00 until 7.35pm, when he made the first of several calls on patients, all situated in the main street, close to his house. Evidence showed, however, that there was a window between 7.15 and 7.50, when his movements were secret. It *was* tight, but the presumption is that he engineered a second tryst with his victim between 7.30 and 7.35pm and was back at a patient's house at 7.50. The clock that was slow was nearly his undoing.

To look at the evidence more closely: at 7.15pm, Elspeth McPherson was on her way to fetch water from a well, and she recognised Dr Smith near the cartwright's shop, 'walking slowly towards Black Dikes Road'. Two other witnesses also placed him near the cartwright's at the same time. Dr Smith was proved to have spent one hour at the Free Church Manse, from 'about' 6.00pm to 7.00pm, attending a sick servant. He had not been expected. Then, he said, he went straight home, where he brought in some dahlia roots from the garden. Next, he said, he left home at 7.35pm to visit a patient, Miss Isabella Anderson, and there he took up a candle to look at the clock, and drew Miss Anderson's attention to the time – 7.35pm. What he did not anticipate was that she would later swear that the clock was a quarter of an hour slow, and therefore he did not arrive until 7.50pm.

After about five minutes, during which he did not sit down,

(but she saw nothing untoward in his appearance or demeanour) he moved on to visit Mr and Mrs Pirie (he was the village farrier). Here he stayed only two minutes saying that he had to see Mrs Manson, who lived over the way, and would shortly return, which he did, after some ten minutes. (He was keeping on the move, to baffle enquiry.) Mr Pirie offered him a seat by the fire because it was raining heavily, but after first taking it, he rose and took one 'far back at the side'.

Over at the Mansons', the doctor was not expected. Mrs Manson had given birth to a baby earlier that day, and was surprised to see him. He moved his chair behind her, and sat down without taking off his hat. She thought that he did not want her to look at him. He did not stay long and afterwards she said to her husband that she did not know what was the matter with Dr Smith – he kept wiping his face and she thought that his nose was bleeding.

While under arrest at Robertson's inn, before removal to Peterhead, the doctor made a determined attempt to pervert the course of justice, by instructing the landlady's daughter, in a whisper, to go to Miss Isabella Anderson (whose clock was slow) and ask her if she could remember that it was 7.35pm when he called on her. If she could remember that, 'everything would be all right'. But, said Miss Anderson, she understood that she was wanted to say something different from the truth, and she would not be swayed.

On the Sunday, while still a free man, the doctor had leaned heavily upon William Fraser, who rang the 8 o'clock curfew at the church every night and therefore had a particular awareness of time. He it was who was a principal witness as to the timing of the shot at 7.35pm. The doctor listened as he told his tale to the constable, and returned later on his own and asked the bellman if it would not be at 7.45pm that he had heard the report.

The doctor's servants did their best for him. Martha Cadger said that she let her master in between 7.25 and 7.30pm, and that ten minutes later he went out by the back door to the offices. She followed him out to feed the pig, and saw him in the garden with a spade. He came home at 9 o'clock and the next morning she saw some dahlia roots in the house which had not been there on the Saturday.

Eliza Park was not so helpful. She, too, said that her master came in at 7.30pm and went out again in ten minutes, but she admitted that the house clock was five or ten minutes fast. Some dahlias were brought in on the Sunday. Alexander Dugid (a follower?) who was in the kitchen that evening, said he left to go home at 7.45pm. He heard the doctor's step in the passage at about 7.30pm.

The trial of Dr William Smith took place in Edinburgh, occupying the 12th to 14th April 1854. A first, void, trial had begun on March 13th, but on the second day it had been halted because one of the jurymen had been 'overcome by mental excitement' and had been certified as unfit to continue his duties. This must have been an interesting spectacle. The defence produced a surprise witness, last on in the case. This was Adam Gray, described for extra probity as 'brother to the Provost of Peterhead' and he was brought to show that, in spite of the denial of the whole clan of McDonalds, William *had* been in possession of a pistol, in fact the pistol at issue. On September 15th 1848, William had asked him, 'You pick up things at roups [auctions] – have you no gun that you could sell me?' Gray asked if he was going to poach, but he said that it was to frighten rooks from the crops (which would be more in character). Gray then sold him a 'useless' pistol for 4s. 6d., which he identified as the pistol exhibited in court by a notch on the stock. Gray's documentary evidence as to the sale proved somewhat shaky. There was some blustering. 'Everyone keeps a jotter as he likes,' he suggested. 'It may be a queer book, but it is true.' It turned out that he had a previous conviction for firing a gun at a trespasser.

William's mother did some serious damage to the defence by recounting that William had told her that Dr Smith had forbidden him to tell anyone about their meetings. When her son met the doctor at his stable door in the evening at 'bell-ringing' there was a mark set on the door to show that the doctor would be coming to the tryst. Evidence that Dr Smith had been seen, a few weeks before the death, practising with a pistol near that stable door did him no good at all.

The Lord Justice-Clerk, however, would have none of it. He charged the jury that it had not been substantiated that murder had actually been committed. He attached importance to the evidence of the brother to the Provost of Peterhead. The doctors could not say if murder or suicide lay behind the shooting. The pistol had not been proved to belong to Dr Smith. Thus instructed, after a bare ten minutes, the jury returned a verdict of Not Proven by a majority. Four had been for Guilty. Hisses in the crowded court-room demonstrated public opinion and the doctor, after a strategic delay, left the building with some difficulty. He did try to get the insurance companies to pay out, but they resisted him and the actions were abandoned. So common is the name of William Smith (and he might have changed it, anyway) that it would be arduous to discover how long he lived on and practised, unshriven.

CHAPTER 11
THE WILD GEESE

The unwanted wife, wrongly incarcerated in an asylum, has, of late, been a subject for study. Some, but not all, of the attention has been of Feminist hue. John Sutherland, in *Victorian Fiction* (Macmillan, 1995) shows that Thackeray, Dickens and Lytton all arranged to have their wives put away, with the connivance of pliable alienists. Mrs Georgina Weldon, formidable 'Plaintiff in Person', who escaped the attempt in 1878 to take her away, was a fine example. She sued and sued the whole lot of them – certifying physicians, asylum proprietor, and family friend who signed the statutory order – and won substantial damages. She had been vulnerable, because she was a spiritualist, and much was made in court of her having had a pet rabbit which had 'appeared' at a séance. Mrs Elizabeth Saunders fits well, one might say, into a line of wives subject to masculine conspiracy.

Her husband, John Saunders, five years her junior, was a gamekeeper of Mellors-ish aspect, a tall, well-built man of fresh complexion, popular with sporting men of the neighbourhood, and thought of as a good fellow. In 1913, the year when things went wrong, he was 32 and she was 37. They lived at Gosford West Lodge, on the Gosford House estate, East Lothian, by the Firth of Forth, where he was in the employment of the Earl of Wemyss. Lodge houses are only miniature mansions, however handsomely decorated, and at this particular doll's-house, a most peculiar domestic set-up had evolved. There were just two bedrooms: in one, slept the gamekeeper, in the other, the wife, her aged mother, and the wife's 21-year-old niece, who had been co-opted to do the housework. John Saunders resented this bizarre arrangement and his anger shows in a remark to his mother-in-law that he was nothing but a lodger in his own home. He was not the master of the doll's-house.

The basic problem that gnawed at the marriage was the long-standing, intractable, intermittent neurotic illness of the wife. Make no mistake, she was ill, but it was not a madness. John Saunders had known her for years before they were married on May 24th 1901, and he took her on in the full knowledge that she was 'delicate' and in the habit of consulting doctors. He could not complain that he had been deceived, and it could have been that very 'delicacy' which attracted him. No doubt he thought that marriage would cure her.

Elizabeth Saunders was a very neurotic woman indeed, and she showed many classic symptoms of anxiety: panic attacks, hypochondriasis, feelings of weakness, a sense of impending doom, depression and a spoilt enjoyment of life, fretful dissatisfaction with the status quo, especially where she lived, and (a minor indication) bolting her food. Not all her days were bad, and good external factors could relieve the stress and lift her mood. She was not easy to live with and an exceptionally patient husband was needed. Anxiety was not much rated in those days, and doctors faced with a miserable female patient of this type leaned heavily on the vague diagnosis of 'neurasthenia'. Hysteria in its true sense of the production of 'conversion symptoms' arising from unconscious drive to seek attention was recognised, and there probably was an element of hysteria in Elizabeth's illness.

Psychiatry was none too hot in the early 1920s, and the treatment prescribed for her was quite antiquated, with a reliance on sedation by bromide. (Not that Valium would have done her any good!) It was no wonder that she could not get up in the morning and dust the doll's-house, as she lay there, pole-axed by sedation and depression. She and Freud would have had a field day, analysing the root cause of her problems. The most effective of the series of doctors who tried to treat her adopted a reassuring, paternalistic approach. This was helpful. Others who took a tough line, implying that she was lazy, malingering, 'introspective', too taken up with herself, and ought to snap out of it, naturally got nowhere.

The marriage was childless, but the husband was eager, although it was awkward to articulate such things, to indicate that 'marital relations' were still in place. The wife would have had to drift into, or be persuaded into, what should have been the matrimonial bedroom. Perhaps it was thought that she was not strong enough to bear children. By the age of 37, suffering from 'bad teeth' and 'dyspepsia', she was beginning to be classified as 'of a certain age' by doctors who thronged to write her off.

As her outbursts of frustration and blame, interpreted as 'bad temper', showed no sign of improvement, it is hardly surprising that the gamekeeper took to staying out late at night, which caused her further anxiety and a modicum of suspicion. He had excellent innocent reasons for absence. He was in the Reserve, and went regularly to Aberlady to shoot. He was a conscientious worker, known to the factor of the estate to be out on duty at night more than any other keeper at Gosford. He was often after the wild geese (presumably to drive them away). Elizabeth objected when he went off on his bicycle on Wednesday and Saturday nights and had given up asking where he was going. She lay awake worrying that something would happen to him. He always said it was work.

In defence, he began a campaign of criticism, complaining about her extravagance over food. He attacked her about the presence of her niece, who had been with them for a year, not believing that she herself did not feel up to the housework. The mother's presence he seems to have tolerated better. Actual, overt quarrels, heard by others, were beginning to break out, and, in fact, they had – when they confronted it – been on bad terms for quite a while.

Some hand began now in January, 1913, to sprinkle

strychnine into this cauldron of discontent. The niece, Mary Douglas Chirnside, noticed it first. Her daily duty was to prepare trays for her aunt and grandmother, and to take them up breakfast in bed. The gamekeeper would usually be hanging around the kitchen while this was going on. Only Elizabeth took toast. Perhaps her mother was too edentulous. Only Elizabeth appears to have eaten marmalade. Maybe all the others ate porridge. It makes sense. Little pots of cream, too, were on special daily order for Elizabeth alone.

One morning, the breakfast menu included bread, already spread with marmalade from a jar in the kitchen, and the niece noticed an untoward white powder on the slice. She tasted it, and found that it was bitter, but when she asked the husband to taste the marmalade, he said there was nothing wrong with it. She decided not to take that piece of bread up to her aunt and laid it aside. She did not know what became of it. On January 17th, Elizabeth sat up in bed and toyed with her breakfast of toast, bread and butter and tea, but she did not much enjoy it because there was a 'very nasty bitter taste' on her toast.

The next morning, a Sunday, she could not eat the toast, because it was so bitter, and she felt annoyed. She wondered if the gas cinders which had been used to toast the bread might have caused the funny flavour. Her niece agreed that it tasted bitter. On Wednesday, the 22nd, it happened again. Her niece brought her just half a slice of buttered toast, and she ate part of it. When she got up, she felt sick, shaky, and very giddy, so she took some baking soda in hot water and vomited up a quantity of white, frothy matter. She had no idea what was wrong, and did not even feel particularly under the weather or depressed.

The following day, a horrible and dramatic scene occurred. She ate some of the toast, felt the bitterness for the fourth time, ate some bread and jam and drank her tea, but the tea was exceedingly bitter and she did not drain the cup. Three minutes later, her legs went numb, with a sensation of twisting. Then there came a shaking, and a strange feeling in her back, and a choking in her throat. She had to grip the back of her neck with her hand. Her top set of false teeth were out, and her lower teeth became fixed in her upper gums. She could not open her mouth. She wanted to vomit. There were twitchings in her body, which kept recurring if she moved. Down below in the kitchen, Mary heard a knock, and went upstairs to find her aunt rigid, with her head thrown back and her mouth clamped shut. She seized Mary in a fierce hold, and could not let go. There were three attacks, and then she vomited frothy stuff and felt some relief although quite prostrate and weak. Mary telegraphed for her aunt's usual doctor, Dr Millar of Tranent, but he was not able to attend immediately and sent his assistant, Dr Gamble, who did not arrive until the evening. What he saw was an hysterical person, in a nervous condition, not seriously ill, and he prescribed bromide. The patient said never a word about twitchings or spasms.

The next morning, Dr Millar himself arrived. He had treated Mrs Saunders for seven years and was confident that he could handle her. She suffered from nervous depression and he was used to her complaints. She did look as if she had had a bad turn. She threw up her hands and said that she had been poisoned. He thought this was pure imagination and advised her to put the idea right out of her mind, but he thought her condition grave enough to engage a resident nurse.

Nurse Elizabeth Ellen Cameron of East Linton arrived on Friday, the 24th. She was a good choice, an excellent qualified nurse of the East Lothian Nursing Association, and she had the advantage of knowing the patient from a previous nervous illness, so that she could compare the present symptoms. There had to be a change in the sleeping arrangements: she slept with her patient, mother and niece moved into the husband's bedroom, and husband slept in the kitchen. Nurse found Mrs Saunders in a state of collapse and she did not allow her to go downstairs to the kitchen for a fortnight. Meanwhile, the nurse listened carefully to her patient, who told her about the bitter toast, and in consequence of what she had heard, she tasted the marmalade in its jar in the kitchen, and found it bitter. She took a sample and gave it to Dr Millar when he visited again. A new jar of marmalade was obtained and the husband complained that the first jar had not been emptied.

Nurse Cameron was also suspicious about some wheaten biscuits, bought specially for the patient. They were in a box on the mantelshelf in the kitchen and she thought they had been tampered with. On February 8th, when she was back on her feet, Elizabeth felt like trying a biscuit, and took one from the box. She saw that there was a glistening white powder on it, which looked like baking powder, and she hid it behind a shutter in her mother's bedroom. When her husband asked for proof that her food was being interfered with, she produced the biscuit and broke off a bit for him to taste. He said there was nothing wrong with it. Nurse gave one of the biscuits to Dr Millar; it appeared to him to have been scraped, and there was a white powder on it. He, too, was becoming suspicious.

Then there was the special cream. Twice, after the bottle had been left in the cupboard for some time, the nurse and the niece found it so bitter that they poured it down the sink. This was before Mrs Saunders was allowed downstairs. On the first day that she did come down, the nurse took some cream out of the bottle for the patient as soon as she received it from the milkman, and replaced the bottle with the residue in the cupboard. Two hours later, the nurse and the niece found it to be bitter, and they could see that it had been shaken up. This bottle was given to the doctor. The nurse swore that Mrs Saunders was not in the kitchen during that two-hour period. The portions of cream saved for her were 'perfectly all right'.

Dr Millar communicated with the police, and the suspect samples were taken to Dr Sydney Smith and Professor Harvey Littlejohn at Edinburgh University for analysis. They found about a third of a grain of strychnine in total in the spoilt cream, the one biscuit, the marmalade sample taken by the nurse, and the top layer of the first jar of marmalade. The quantity of poison found 'was not usually accounted a fatal dose, but it was a dangerous one and had caused death'. The strychnine present was, however, only the tip of the iceberg when we consider the amount taken by Mrs Saunders, put in the cream, and scattered on the other wheaten biscuits, where it glittered sinisterly in the gaslight. The fatal dose is usually given as from half to two grains.

John Saunders was arrested and his superiors and colleagues were 'dumbfoundered'. Dr Gamble, alerted by his previous failure to spot anything seriously amiss, made a thorough search of the house for poison and found Rodine (the rat poison containing phosphorus), but no strychnine. The police, of course, were on the same track, but could find no evidence of purchase of strychnine by Saunders. He denied ever possessing, handling, or using strychnine. It was quite customary for gamekeepers to buy strychnine against vermin. It was, in fact, the poison associated with gamekeepers. George Little Bell, Gosford Kennels' head gamekeeper, had some relevant information: he himself had taken over from the late William Saunders, (John Saunder's father), a quantity of strychnine which he kept in a safe place. He had never given any of it out to John Saunders.

The trial of the gamekeeper for the attempted murder of his wife began on April 23rd 1913, in the High Court of Justiciary at Edinburgh. The proceedings were remarkable for the unusual counterbalance between the evidence of the alleged victim, who had found the inner strength to speak out, without actually accusing her husband, and to perform well, and between the accused, who gave evidence on his own behalf and was notably confident. The force of the trial was the endeavour by the defence to blame the wife herself for the plague of strychnine. The trial became, in effect, a kind of Commission in Lunacy, with a procession of male doctors called to construct the impression that the wife was a near-insane hysteric. They argued that Mrs Saunders, in order to blame her husband for making her ill, or to make him move elsewhere, or to stop him from staying out late at night, and to keep her niece, either feigned (rather well) the symptoms of strychnine poisoning, having somehow got hold of a medical textbook, or produced a genuine hysterical fit for the same reasons, but at an unconscious level.

There was a suggestion that, having scattered strychnine abroad, she never actually ingested any of it. Where she was supposed to have got hold of the poison was not hazarded. Although a gamekeeper's wife might be thought to be in a stronger position to hold strychnine than the wife of a village postman, the husband denied ever having it. The defence could not have it both ways. It was implied, although not seriously argued, that she had secretly crept down the stairs while supposedly half-lifeless in her bed, in order to get at the cream. An even more bizarre accusation was that she *had* purposively taken in enough strychnine to produce the symptoms, having the scientific acumen to gauge the dosage to a nicety, or, in the alternative, had taken it recklessly, being of suicidal disposition at the best of times.

One thinks of the Hay poisoning case of 1922, in which Mrs Katherine Armstrong, slowly poisoned by arsenic, was placed in Barnwood Asylum. Her husband, Major Herbert Rowse Armstrong, convicted of her murder (although it has recently been strongly argued that he was innocent) fostered the belief that she was deluded and hypochondriacal, a self-doser.

Early in the Saunders trial, the defence strategy began to unfold as Elizabeth Saunders was cross-examined. She 'could not say' that a dread of being poisoned was one of her long-standing anxieties. She certainly had had a previous experience of poisoning from an accidental overdose of a medicine, and she had since been very careful to look at the directions on medicine bottles. Although under strong pressure, she did manage to slip in the comment that during their 12 years of marriage, her husband had seemed to take a delight in tormenting her and in teasing her about her bad health. Wasn't he trying to stiffen her up and take more interest in life? (counsel asked). Perhaps, she allowed.

The doctors who attended her (counsel took her on) were very firm with her. Her husband had told her that Dr Martine of Haddington had told him that she was lazy. She gave that doctor up in 1906. When she had asked him to prescribe something to brace her up, he had said that it was best to let nature do its own work. She admitted that she was very easily vexed, and often felt apprehensive that some calamity was going to befall her. Over the years, she had taken a lot of medicine, but only what was prescribed. When Dr Gamble called, she did not tell him about her frightening convulsion because he told her that she had worked herself up into such a state, and if she were in the Infirmary, she would have a screen put round her bed, and would not be allowed to worry. She felt that if she told him the facts, he would tell her that it was all nervousness, and she did not like to be spoken to in such terms.

However hard she was pressed, she would not admit to any suicidal thoughts. It was true that she had walked out of the house one night after some 'dispeace' but she did not make for the seashore, only towards her brother's house. One Sunday morning, after some words, she had left home for Boglehill, intending to reach the tram and go to her sister in Edinburgh. On reflection, however, she had realised that it would be selfish to leave her aged mother stranded in her husband's house, and had gone back to the Lodge. Her mind was *not* full of the fear of poison when she thought the toast was bitter: as a matter of fact she was thinking of going to a ball at Aberlady at the time.

Her husband had sometimes put pepper and salt in her food 'for fun'. She wanted to leave Gosford, but her husband would not do so, saying that he had a comfortable place there. She could not remember shouting and screaming at nights, but she did remember a 'seizure' of some kind, four years previously, which had greatly distressed her. Whether she had twitchings on that occasion, she would not say. Once, in an electric tram in Dundee she had indeed become nervous because of the high wind: there was a scene and she had to get out. She had not said in 1912 that some day her husband would find her in the sea, and she could not remember his ever swearing at her.

Nurse Cameron, cross-examined after her powerful account of the discovery of the adulterated food, was asked about the previous illness, in the summer of 1912, when Mrs Saunders woke up one morning convinced that something dreadful was going to happen to her, suffered from horrid dreams, and wanted to leave Gosford, where she was not happy. During the last illness her patient had shown less self-control than in the previous one. Once, Mrs Saunders did go downstairs at night when her husband was out; she seemed to be worrying about him. In fact, she always worried about her husband when he was out late, because his job could be dangerous.

The first doctor in the witness-box was Dr Gamble and he was anxious to tell the court that he had informed Dr Millar that he had found, at that first visit, some symptoms which he could not account for: the patient told him that she was afraid of something coming over her, and she lacked the will power to conquer it. She would not tell him what she was afraid of. Dr Millar, under cross-examination, revealed that Mrs Saunders had asked him if there were any risk that she might do something to herself. She mentioned a friend who had drowned herself: was she likely to do that? He had reassured her. (So her poison phobia and her suicide phobia – if they amounted to that – were now strongly before the court.)

There were times, Dr Millar testified, when Mrs Saunders was on the border line between sanity and insanity, but she was now improving in health. Nervous patients often imagined their symptoms and things that did not exist. If the person who put the poison on the biscuit meant it to be consumed by somebody else, he went very poorly about his business: the thing was so apparent. This comment was a godsend to the defence. The doctor was not asked about the cream on these lines, presumably because the tampering was not 'apparent' in that agent. He was re-examined as to his imputation of insanity, and moderated his opinion as attached to a previous illness, two years previously.

Professor Harvey Littlejohn, for the Crown, said that he had heard the evidence and was of the opinion that all the symptoms spoken of by Mrs Saunders were indicative of poisoning by an overdose of strychnine. Taken altogether, no doctor could attribute such symptoms merely to hysteria. Somehow, though, the defence managed to get him to say that he had never known a murder case where the dose of strychnine (0.323 grain) was so remarkably small. This seems past the point and may not have been accurately reported. *Saunders* was a case of *attempted* murder and the crime charged reflected an ongoing course of conduct. Apart from the quantity of strychnine already destroyed or lost before analysis of the samples, if the case had proceeded to the full charge, obviously chemical analysis of Mrs Saunder's organs would have yielded a higher figure.

The case for the Crown was closed, and the defence began its full-scale attack on the mental responsibility of the wife. Dr Martine was the physician who had attended her in 1905 and 1906, and whose services she had dispensed with, finding him unsympathetic. Her diagnosis was hypochondriasis, he said now uncompromisingly, and he prescribed Valerian (which used to be specifically prescribed for hysteria, often in combination with bromide). On his last visit, he told her that she had better get up: there was plenty to do in the house. He formed the opinion that the husband treated his wife most kindly; he was more than patient, and there was an extraordinary demand on his patience. The Reverend Dr McEwen, parish minister of Gladsmuir, spoke of the accused's kindness and courtesy to the wife, and the reassuring fact that he was a total abstainer. He considered that Mrs Saunders was a very nervous and excitable woman. After this rather un-ministerial comment, the Crown extracted the information that Saunders was not, as it happened, a member of his congregation. Dr Johnstone, another assistant to Dr Millar, was cautious. He used the word 'introspective'. When he saw Mrs Saunders in April 1912, she was worse. The husband was quite good to her.

On the second day of the trial, a consultant, Dr George Lovell Gulland, testified that on October 11th 1905, he was called in to examine Mrs Saunders by the then *locum tenens* of Dr Martine. His evidence referred to a *previous* illness and was extremely adverse to her. He had found the patient to be of poor physique, bad mental balance, hysterical, too much interested in her own symptoms, hypochondriacal, but with a substratum of real defect. That is, for instance, she had bad teeth and bolted her food. But on top of this, there was considerable mental debility.

He would be quite prepared to say that when he first examined Mrs Saunders she was on the border line between sanity and insanity. His view was confirmed when he saw her again later. A woman in such a condition tended to think that the world centred in her. Her whole object was to draw attention and sympathy to herself. Such a condition was apt to prevail at a certain period in life. If an hysterical woman had once read or heard of the symptoms of poisoning by strychnine, it would be quite possible for her to simulate these by suggestion. A person in a real fit of strychnine rigidity would seize another person or an object, but would be far too rigid to let go during the continuance of the fit. (But it was in evidence that when her niece came up to see what was wrong, Mrs Saunders gripped hold of her and could not relax her grip.)

Cross-examined, he said that Mrs Saunders was treated in the Chalmers Hospital, Edinburgh, for three weeks in 1906. Dr Gulland had not been in court during Mrs Saunders' examination (as he had demonstrated). The Solicitor-General then read out to him the evidence relating to the symptoms and he agreed that they did resemble those of strychnine poisoning, with the exception of the fixing of the teeth in the upper jaw. There was no special stiffness or locking of the jaw in strychnine poisoning. It was not to be taken as characteristic of the condition. (An interesting piece of nit-picking! Let us see how well he had remembered his Taylor's *Medical Jurisprudence*. Yes: Taylor has a differential table with strychnine set against tetanus and in strychnine the illness 'Does not commence in, nor especially affect, the jaw'.)

Dr Sillar, assistant to Sir Thomas Fraser, Edinburgh, gave expert evidence as to the analysis of the samples of food. The Crown cross-examined and elicited opinions which would have been more useful to the defence. He said that he had heard Mrs Saunders give her evidence, and believed that she was not of normal mind. Challenged, he would not say that she struck him as being actually of unsound mind, but he would not concede that she showed no sign of mental instability, although she did seem to testify with clearness and intelligence. In fact, he would prefer not to give any definite opinion as to her mental state. Nor could he offer an opinion that life would have been lost if she had taken the poison stated to have been present in other food in the house.

The final expert witness called by the defence to destroy the credibility of Mrs Saunders was a consultant psychiatrist of some eminence, Sir Thomas Smith Clouston, born on Orkney, 1840, and soon to die in 1915. His appointments included Physician Superintendent of the Royal Asylum, Morningside, Edinburgh, and Medical Superintendent of the Cumberland and Westmorland Asylums. He stated that he had a long and wide experience of nervous and neurotic conditions, and had heard the evidence in the case. He had not been given the opportunity to examine Mrs Saunders professionally and had had to be content with observing her in the witness-box.

His views on hysteria had a punitive tone. He said that she described the outstanding symptoms of that illness. A certain want of truthfulness and candour were also characteristic. The fear of impending calamity was of the nature of an insane delusion. (This was undoubtedly an old-fashioned view.) Hysterical women would do almost anything to excite sympathy. *It appeared to him that the nurse in this case had been watching the wrong person: she should have watched the patient.* He thought that there was a strong possibility of Mrs Saunders carrying out such a scheme as might here be suggested. He was cross-examined forcefully and admitted that he could not say that Mrs Saunders exhibited neurotic signs in the witness-box, but it had to be borne in mind that hysterics were often able to behave in an apparently normal way. *He considered it strongly probable that Mrs Saunders used strychnine to excite sympathy for herself.* He noticed one significant thing: she left the box with a self-satisfied smile on her face. 'Did she now?' the Solicitor-General mocked him. 'Well, I didn't see it, and I don't think the jury saw it either. It must have been meant for you, Sir Thomas, as you were sitting beside the box!' The courts had never been receptive to the opinion of alienists, but what was that to the male jury and the crowd of Saunders' supporters who had come into Edinburgh from the country. The damage had been done, and Mrs Saunders, her reputation in tatters, was presented as some kind of dangerous, scheming lunatic.

The gamekeeper strode into the witness-box, a manly figure, sure of himself. He was led through his contention that his wife was suicidal, which she had denied. She often said that she would do something to herself. On the occasion of her previously mentioned exit down by Boglehill to the shore, her mother asked him to follow her, keeping out of sight. Three-quarters of a mile from home, she suddenly retraced her footsteps. He facetiously asked her if the water had been too cold for her – rather a grim jest, he conceded – and she said, 'I will do it some day'. Whenever she heard of a suicide, she became frightened and dwelt on it. She bucked up on hearing that she might inherit some property. He thought that she was not strong enough to go to the ball at Aberlady. He tried some of the marmalade and thought it had a horrid smell, with a little speck of white on it. His wife took a biscuit from behind a shutter. He tasted it and after going downstairs felt a clammy taste in his mouth and a burning in his throat, but he did not tell his wife so, because it struck him that there was some underhand plot in the house to put him in blame.

The summing-up leaned towards the accused – 'The question of Not Guilty or Not Proven might be of great moment to a man in the position of the accused' – and the gamekeeper was unanimously found Not Guilty. He was rapturously received with cheers and handshakes. Mrs Saunders flew free from the Lodge for a new life elsewhere, and later her husband divorced her on the grounds of her desertion. The decree was granted by Lord Ormidale, the same judge who had sat at his criminal trial. Under the new law, no doubt Saunders would have put forward his wife's 'unreasonable behaviour'.

CHAPTER 12
THE FRENCH
SCHOOLMASTER'S WIFE

Eugène Marie Chantrelle was an incendiarist of the mind, sizzling with fantasies of blowing the whole lot of them to Kingdom Come, and in particular his mother-in-law in her house at 5 Buccleuch Place, Edinburgh, and in general, 'Would that I [he said] could but place a fuse in the centre of this earth, that I could blow it to pieces, and with it the whole of humanity! I hate them!'

This new Guy Fawkes, a Frenchman, was a failed doctor, born in 1834 at Nantes, where he attended medical school. When his father's shipping business foundered, he became erratic, attending classes at Strasbourg and Paris, but never qualifying, although he surely thought that he was just as good as any registered practitioner. His taste for violence and arson was formed, no doubt, at the barricades in Paris during the *coup d'état* of 1851, where he received a sabre-wound in the arm. As he had espoused the wrong, Republican side, he withdrew to America where his doings are unknown. He will have been up to no good.

Chantrelle was a priapic man, fully capable of rape, as afterwards came to light. When he descended on Edinburgh in 1866, however, he was still guarding his reputation and the respectable citizens gladly accepted him as a schoolmaster, even entrusting their adolescent daughters to his care. Textbooks and primers on French and Latin flowed from his pen and he was considered an ornament to the cultural life of the city. At first there was an air, a style about him, and he was of good continental address. One who observed him noted that he was a 'powerfully-built, square-shouldered, good-looking, cultured man. He had finely-cut features, with a moustache and mutton-chop whiskers and a good crop of well-trimmed hair'. He spoke near-perfect idiomatic English, with a fascinating French accent. None knew that he had already had a conviction in England for an outrage 'of a very gross nature' upon one of his pupils, and had served a sentence of nine months' imprisonment.

Newington Academy, in Arniston Place, was one of the private schools where Chantrelle taught French. In 1867, a pupil, Elizabeth Cullen Dyer, aged 15, the daughter of a commercial traveller, attended his classes. By her photographs, she was a beauty, with long golden hair, and when, perhaps, she was 16, Chantrelle seduced her. This was no rape: extant early letters show that she was as besotted by her exotic lover as Madeleine Smith by Pierre Emile L'Angelier ten years previously. Pregnancy came as a bombshell, and, against his nature, Chantrelle allowed himself to be manoeuvred into marriage. He had not been netted before and the best explanation for his compliance is that he was still intent on making a go of it in Edinburgh. Otherwise, he would have decamped without a qualm.

The wedding took place on August 11th 1868, when he was 34 and she was 17. In a photograph, taken soon afterwards, she is large and miserable and he is saturnine. Her mouth turns down in a rictus of foreboding. A respectable household was set up at 81a George Street, his bachelor quarters, where in conditions which became somewhat cramped, they occupied a parlour, dining-room, kitchen and 'class-room' on one floor, and two bedrooms, a servant's bedroom, closet and bathroom above. Chantrelle strutted a bit, swollen with the importance of his new situation in life. There was always a maid (once he had had a black manservant) and he became a Freemason. (Well, he said so, and, to be more particular, a member of the Red Cross Knight Order of Masons.)

Baby No. 1, Eugène John, was born on October 22nd 1868, delivered by Chantrelle himself. Madame Chantrelle (her girlish identity lost so soon) usually nursed her babies for one month, but not her first-born. Probably a wet-nurse was employed, and then unpasteurised cow's milk was offered. One son did not survive. Louis was born in 1871, and 'the baby' was born on December 6th, 1876. There was thus no failure of 'marital relations' but the marriage, as a relationship, was a total failure. We should now call it an abusive one. The dapper, muscled husband raged with explosive fire in the trap which he had not sought and began to strike out in anger. The wife was seen with a black eye; he threw a candlestick at her and threatened to 'smash' the children and make mincemeat of her.

He drank heavily and we should say now that he was an alcoholic. His maid knew that he drank a bottle of whisky a day at home, and since he was not much at home anyway, and had little interest in meal-times, who knows how much more he drank in surroundings which he found more convivial. His breakfast, diagnostically, was one cup of tea with whisky in it. However, these things are cultural, and many a Victorian husband survived on years of drinking to excess, and certainly Chantrelle's famous libido was unimpaired. Far from it. He was a frequent visitor to the brothels of Clyde Street. A detective saw him there.

Gossip about the schoolmaster's two vices was beginning to circulate and business was falling off. He took it out on his wife and repeatedly threatened to poison her by untraceable means. It was a martyrdom. Twice she appealed to the police for protection, and sometimes went home to Mamma but always returned. She consulted a lawyer about a divorce, but nothing came of it. Her uncle was a doctor and he could have helped her more, but marriage was sacred. Still the raging husband waved his loaded pistol at her and discharged it at the bedroom door for target practice. He shot up the brothels, too, when the mood took him. Behaving badly was his way of life.

Holidays from this tindery ménage were taken at Portobello by the sea and one day in their lodgings, Eugène got hold of Papa's pistol and accidentally discharged it. Louis and Papa were both slightly wounded and the incident turned Chantrelle's mind towards the benefits of insurance payments. It should be said that in 1877 he owed £200 and had 17s. 11d. in the bank. The butcher was pressing him very hard. After first making prudent enquiries as to the exact nature of accidental death in insurance terms, Chantrelle approached another firm, a new one, going under the name of the Accidental Assurance Association of Scotland, and insured the life of his wife for £1,000. 'Mamma,' she said on a visit home, 'my life is insured now and you will see that my life will go soon.' 'Nonsense!' quoth Mamma, 'there's no fears of that.' But still she said, 'I cannot help thinking it; something within me tells me that it will be so.'

One week later, it was Hogmanay at No. 81 George Street, and there was a semblance of truce. Madame had been out and about, buying presents for the children, and posting off greetings cards. Papa was home for supper, for once, and a bottle of champagne was on the table, together with a contribution from Mamma – shortbread and a cake. When midnight struck, all the bands in the Castle garrison began to play, and master and mistress and maid stood at the open window to welcome in the New Year of 1878.

Next morning, Madame woke with a headache and nausea. There has never been an explanation for this malady, whether it was a hangover, migraine (for she did complain to her mother about her headaches) or dosage from husband, by way of a pre-med. Mary Byrne, the Irish maid (illiterate according to Chantrelle) departed on her servant's holiday. Eugène was sent out to buy a duck for supper. Madame vomited a clear fluid like water into the parlour fire. Eugène held her head, as she had often done for him. Somehow, she managed to steam the duck à l'oignon. When Papa rolled in, he sent to the Hanover Hotel for some grapes and four bottles of lemonade. The family dined at 5pm, but Madame could eat nothing at all and retired to bed at 6pm, taking the baby in with her. At 9.45pm, Mary the maid came home and went up to the bedroom. The gas was lighted. Madame was 'very heavy-looking'. She asked Mary to peel an orange for her.

At about midnight (Chantrelle takes up the story) he went up to the other bedroom, where he slept, for various logistical reasons, with the two elder boys, and undressed before venturing into his wife's room. She was still awake, and had been reading the *Family Herald*. There was some matrimonial chit-chat, and some kind of amatory connection. The baby woke up and began to babble. His wife said that she would not be able to sleep and begged him to remove Baby, which he did. He kissed her and left her alone for the night.

Mary the maid crept down from her narrow bed, the next morning at 7am-ish, to make a cup of tea for her mistress. She was about to light the kitchen fire, when she heard a moaning noise, rather like the cat. She ran upstairs and was surprised to find that the gas was out, although it was usually kept burning all night, and that the baby was not, as it should be, in bed with its mother. There was no smell of gas. In the pale daylight, she saw Madame lying white and unconscious, partly on her side on the bed, like Wallis's *The Death of Chatterton*, with her eyelids closed. Intermittently, she emitted a deep moan. There was vomit on her golden hair which seemed to have come out of its usual bedtime plait, and green-brown stuff on the bedclothes.

The frightened girl knocked three times at her master's door and entered. In the small iron bed lay Chantrelle, wide-awake and looking at her, and all three children, squashed together but asleep. She told him what was wrong, and went back to her mistress. He took his time to dress in the bare minimum for decency – his drawers, a flannel shirt, stockings and slippers. He stood at his wife's bedside. The maid suggested a doctor. 'I hear the baby crying,' he said, and sent her out to check. She found that all the children were still fast asleep. The only noise in the house was the terrible, meaningless moaning. She went back to Madame and caught Chantrelle in the act of coming back from the window, as if after raising the bottom sash. Did she not notice a smell of gas? he asked her. She did not, but turned off the meter in the kitchen. The master dressed and went off for a doctor, not the nearest one, too old to be woken at such an early hour, he thought, but young Dr Carmichael of No. 42 Northumberland Street, whom he knew from the Masons.

It was 8.30 in the morning when a real doctor stood at the patient's bedside. His first thought was that she was dying. There was now a strong smell of gas, and they carried her into the other bedroom. They could not find the leak. The doctor wrote a note for delivery to Dr Henry Littlejohn which read: 'If you would like to see a case of coal-gas poisoning [then still a rarity] come up here at once.' The maid was sent for a bottle of brandy to be administered as an enema, a remedy then for heart-failure. Dr Carmichael could not help noticing that the level in the bottle kept going down, as the grieving husband helped himself to it – a coarse gesture, one would have thought, and afterwards held against him.

Dr Littlejohn turned up at 9.30am and found Dr Carmichael desperately trying to produce artificial respiration. He advised removal to the Royal Infirmary, and himself reported the apparent leak of gas to the Gas Company. Mamma arrived, with her own doctor, Dr Gordon of George Square, and he helped Dr Carmichael with artificial respiration. At one stage, Chantrelle was asked to help, but he could not seem to stick to it. At one o'clock, the dying woman was taken to the hospital, where Dr Maclagan, Professor of Medical Jurisprudence, examined her. His immediate opinion was that this was a case of narcotic poisoning, not gas inhalation. There was no smell of coal-gas. There was no pulse at the wrist, and the heartbeat was intermittent. They carried on the artificial respiration and applied another brandy enema and an electrical stimulus, but they knew that it was hopeless. By 4.00pm she was dead. Chantrelle told his hated mother-in-law that they had murdered his wife in the infirmary with their inept treatments. She observed that he did not bother to show distress to her, but then she did not expect him to do so.

The post-mortem took place at the Royal Infirmary on January 3rd, and no cause, absolutely no cause, of death was found. On the 4th, two gas-fitters and a criminal officer went to No. 81a and searched the premises until they found Chantrelle's 'leak'. A bracket had been removed in the architrave of the window of Madame's bedroom, and when they opened the shutter they saw a freshly broken gas pipe. The fracture had obviously been caused by bending the pipe backward and forward, which could have been done very quickly in two turns. Confronted with this evidence, Chantrelle denied any knowledge of the pipe. This was foolish, because another gas-fitter had been called out in August 1876 on report of a leak, and had found an escape of gas from a small hole in precisely that same pipe. He remembered that Chantrelle had watched the operation with interest as he tightened the pipe, remarking with typical philanthropy, 'It must have been that damn dirty German' – apparently a former tenant.

The funeral of Elizabeth Chantrelle at the Grange Cemetery on January 5th was dramatic, pre-Raphaelite even, in its staged perfection. Chantrelle had her buried in her wedding dress, and he made a show of trying to fling himself into the open grave. Those present were naturally surprised but no doubt, except for mother-in-law, thought that guilt over his long course of cruelty had brought about a release of remorse. On his return home, he was arrested for the murder of his wife. Behind the scenes, chemical analysis had been made of stains of vomit on the dead woman's nightdress and sheet, and three-quarters of a grain of opium in solid form had been found, accompanied by portions of grapes and orange. The same fruits had also been recognized in the contents of the stomach.

Thinking now that even if opium might have escaped absorption in the stomach, it might have passed into the intestines, which had not, unaccountably, been retained, the experts arranged an exhumation on January 10th for the purpose of removing the intestines. Yet again, the results of analysis were negative. The investigations made by the police were proving more successful. It turned out that Chantrelle kept a veritable miniature pharmacy in a locked cupboard in his class-room, which contained harmless homeopathic drugs side-by-side with poisons such as arsenic and tartar emetic. On November 25th, 1877, he had bought in from Robertsons' chemists a drachm, i.e. 60 grains of extract of opium comprising 30 doses, each capable of taking a human life. Extract of opium is the stronger form. Most suspiciously, this hoard of opium was nowhere to be found in Chantrelle's den.

As the situation stood, Chantrelle had not been clever enough by half. He had certainly honoured his boast that he could administer poison to his wife in such a way that the whole Faculty of Edinburgh could not detect it, but, though he had had ample time to clear up, he had left stains of poisoned vomit patent for all to see. The faked gas leak was clumsily staged, and should have been done earlier. Bricks of circumstantial evidence grew into a castle, and on 8th and 9th January, the prisoner made his pre-trial declarations. He was beginning to rant and ramble, deprived as he was of his supportive alcohol, and he does not always appear quite sane, although his sanity was never at issue.

The chief burden of his storm of words was that his wife had twice been unfaithful to him – with a bank clerk, and a neighbour – and that he had nobly forgiven her. She had had her 'peculiarities'. Jealousy. Threats of suicide. (Some there were, it is true in her immature love-letters.) He used to find her stooped over her washing tub in the bedroom with her head bent forward and her nose on the edge of the tub, as if about to immerse her face in the water. She read 'penny trashy novels'.

She used to take chloral. (Of which there was a very minute trace in the tissues of the stomach.)

The trial of Eugène Marie Chantrelle at Edinburgh began on May 7th, 1878. The appearance in the witness-box of the eldest son, Eugène, aged nine, a brave manikin, traumatised for life, caused a sensation. He once saw Papa strike Mamma with his hand on the side of her head. Cross-examined, 'My father has always been kind to me. He gave me everything I asked for. He gave me pennies to buy toys, and took me out for walks. On New Year's Day, Papa was kind to Mamma, as far as I saw'.

In general, however, *Chantrelle* was a great medical trial. John Trayner displayed all the brilliance in the defence of the crime which his client had lacked in its commission. Chantrelle was not grateful, and turned on him at one stage: 'Is that all?' he was heard to demand. Little was made of the possibility of suicide. Trayner's brief was to attack the weakest part of the Crown case – the absence of opium in the body. He compared the eight or nine symptoms of opium poisoning as laid down in Taylor's *Medical Jurisprudence* and estimated that five symptoms were 'a' wanting' during the fatal illness: stertorous breathing, profuse perspiration, rattle in the throat at the end, drooping or relaxation of the jaw, and a stronger pulse than was found. He argued that it was impossible to prove that the stains on the night-gown and sheet were actually vomit. (Dr Carmichael, at the scene, had observed that vomited matter was oozing from the mouth.)

Found guilty and sentenced to death, to his evident surprise, Chantrelle was allowed to address the court. He presented a lost and grotesque spectacle, ghastly pale, his whiskers fanned out more sparsely than of yore, gesticulating, losing the thread, his voice rising higher and higher. Still showing off his superior medical and chemical skills, he shot away at a tangent from his established defence by saying that he was satisfied that opium was found outside the body, but 'It did not proceed from Madame Chantrelle's stomach, but '*was rubbed in by some person for a purpose which I do not know.* I know my word goes for nothing. I don't wish it to go for anything'.

Afterwards, although it was a popular verdict, a public petition was prepared and submitted to the Home Secretary. It was alleged that two members of the jury had been fast asleep, during the judge's summing-up, and that another had been suffering from a form of temporary blindness – amaurosis – which had rendered him incapable of appreciating the written evidence, which was a palpably absurd suggestion. Still scheming, Chantrelle was responsible for the claim that he was 'very poor' and therefore was not adequately defended. He now put forward the alternative theory that his wife had died of kidney disease, and that the kidneys had not been properly examined. Nausea, vomiting and lassitude had been her chronic symptoms. When he discovered his wife beyond medical aid, the new explanation continued, an *evil thought* occurred to him for the first time – he would cheat the insurance company by hurriedly breaking the gas pipe and striving to persuade the medical attendants that her death was not due to natural causes.

All his ingenuity, emanating from a mind cleared of alcohol, was useless, and soon he realized that 'If it is to be, it must be'. They could not get him to admit his crime. When his last night came, he slept well and had to be roused at 5.00am. He enjoyed a light breakfast of coffee and eggs, and was allowed to smoke. Invited to solicit some small extra treat, he caustically suggested, 'Three bottles of champagne and ***.' Knowing his vices, it is only too easy for us to supply the missing words. Fortified with a nip of spirits (brandy perhaps) he gave no trouble as Marwood the hangman pinioned him, and, dressed in his suit of mourning, stoically took part in a short religious service in the chief warder's room. They heard him joining in the singing from the 51st Psalm: 'Purge me with hyssop, and I shall be clean: wash me, and I shall be whiter than snow…Deliver me from blood-guiltiness, O God…a broken and contrite heart, O God, thou wilt not despise...' For some reasons of tact, decency or expediency, the first six verses were omitted. Would he have sung 'For I acknowledge my transgressions: and my sin is ever before me..'? His was the first execution in Scotland to be conducted in private and he was observed to inspect the gallows' equipment with an interested and scientific eye.

The author's husband, Richard Whittington-Egan, treasures amongst his criminous memorabilia a poignant relic – a double linen cuff, Isabella-coloured now, which once belonged to Madame Chantrelle. Another rare item in the collection is a volume specially bound for Chantrelle in red leather, entitled *Pleasures of Literature* by Robert Aris Wilmott (Bell and Daldy, 186 Fleet Street, 1860). Across the outside front cover, *COURS DE M. CHANTRELLE* is tooled in gilt letters. Inside appears the hand-written inscription 'IInd Prize 1st Class, Awarded to Miss ****** Session 1869-1870. E. Chantrelle'. The embarrassed donee had later obliterated her own name.

Richard Whittington-Egan discovered documents which charge Chantrelle with full rape. In a letter (preserved in Edinburgh's Central Library) Miss Ellen Lucy Holme wrote from Cromer on July 1st, 1867:

Dear Mr Chantrelle,
I am very much annoyed at being obliged to write to you, but as you are the only one who can help me out of my trouble, I am compelled to do so. You cannot have forgotten what happened in your house on the 1st of January, and how you quieted my fears by assuring me that nothing would result from what you had done, which I in my simplicity fully believed, but now I find that you must have been deceiving me all the time, if not yourself as well. You cannot be surprised when I tell you that I expect to be confined in three months' time, and you, and you only, are the father of the child. I have left my situation

(as governess) for my holidays, but in the state I find myself, I cannot possibly return...'

The desperate letters from the betrayed governess somehow got into the hands of the prosecution during preparations for the trial of Chantrelle, and she was traced to a different address in Norfolk. A proof was taken from her, dated February 2nd, 1878, ten years after the outrage. She was now a spinster of 38, and she stated: 'My father is a clergyman in the Church of England and resides at Dawlish in Devonshire. I was not happy at home. My stepmother was not kind. We then resided in Edinburgh. I resolved to look for a situation as a governess. One day my stepmother taunted me by saying that no-one would have me. I then determined I would take any situation rather than remain at home. After this I saw an advertisement in, I think, an Edinburgh paper for a housekeeper, not a governess, and to apply personally at 81 George Street...

'I said to the servant who opened the door that I had come about the advertisement. I was shown into a large front room (the dining-room) where a gentleman was whom I afterwards knew as Mr Chantrelle. He seemed to avoid the subject of a housekeeper. He began to sympathize with me and I was at the time so very unhappy at home that anyone who spoke kindly to me at once drew my heart. I never dreamt of any danger. He drew me to him and before I could realize anything, he threw me down forcibly on the floor. I resisted as much as I could but he was very strong and evidently carried away by his passions. I screamed out, too, and he said, "Hush. Hush." I was dreadfully frightened and have always been very nervous. He put his hand on my mouth. He then had forcible connection with me while he held me down. He said, "You will come again, won't you?" I had of course then seen that he never wanted a housekeeper. Before he forced me, he had asked me to take some claret, but I would not, I have always felt since that I should never have gone. I had not the least idea that the advertisement was not in good faith.'

Her son, born on September 22nd, 1867, (one year before the Chantrelle marriage) at Cromer was 'very like his father'. She had supported herself partly by teaching and her father gave her an allowance. Which was worse, to be the legitimate child of Eugène Marie Chantrelle, or not even to bear his name?

CHAPTER 13
THE ICE-FIELD

Time has etched out some of the layers of sadness in the strange, forgotten case of the boy stowaways on the cargo ship *Arran*. Looking back now, wincing at the tale of cruelty, the boys' forced trek on the ice-fields off Newfoundland has in the mind's eye the pictorial quality of some epic Arctic film. Whether the cruelty, which reads like outright torture, amounted to pathological sadism is doubtful. The year was 1868. Ocean-going ships were not known for their humane discipline, and a fierce dominance kept down the ever-present threat of mutiny. On land, poor boys, waifs and strays – burnt chimney sweeps, maimed infant mill-workers, Dr Barnardo's ragged destitutes found huddled in rows under the tarpaulins on roofs – were exploited and expendable. Whether the final harsh act which led to two deaths at sea should have been tried as murder, not reduced, as it was, to manslaughter, is a different matter. We should probably regard it as murder.

Bound for Quebec, on April 7th 1868, the *Arran* set sail from the great port of Greenock, on the south bank of the Clyde. A wooden sailing ship of 1063 tons register, she was laden with coal and oakum, that being, since we have lost touch with these things, hempen fibre, made from old ropes, and used for caulking ships' seams. A full crew of 22 were under Robert Watt, captain, aged 28, of Saltcoats, in Ayrshire, and his brother-in-law, James Kerr, mate, aged 31, of Lochranza, Isle of Arran. Both men were of fierce, commanding aspect, bearded like the pard, but not of identical disposition: the captain was supposed to be weak, dominated by the vicious mate.

After the tug had gone back, and they were well out to sea, too late to return them to shore, seven unwelcome young figures came up blinking from various hiding-places in the bowels of the ship, just in time before the carpenter battened down the hatches for the voyage. It is not clear whether the great adventure was a joint enterprise or merely an ill-omened coincidence. At least two of the boys knew each other. Seven were too many. Seven extra mouths to feed, and seven useless appendages, too young and weak to work hard for their board. By marine custom and common law you tossed your stowaways a crust and a bone, regularly, and you kept them alive. Seven made up a crew of their own and the very sight of them was an irritant to the bearded ones.

All the stowaways had emerged from the poorest parts of Greenock. Some of them had mothers. Bernard Reilly, aged 22, the eldest, had secreted himself with the express intention of emigrating to Canada in order to find employment. James Bryson, 16, seems to have had what we would now call 'problems', although he was to give evidence very clearly. He was dirty in his person and habits and averse to work. David Brand was also 16. Peter Currie, 12, was in a favoured position, because his father, back home, was friendly with the mate. There remain three really young boys, all aged 11: Hugh McGinnes, Hugh McEwan and John Paul who were already friends. Hugh McEwan was weakly, a consumptive, and spat blood. 'Please, sir,' said one of the 11-year-olds, interrogated by the frowning captain, upon discovery, 'we want to be sailors.'

The boys were thin, undernourished, to start with, and nearly all were dressed in one set of ragged cast-offs, quite unsuited to the hail, frost, snow and continuous rain of the north Atlantic crossing. Some of them were barefooted. No effort was made to provide or improvise other clothing or footwear: the boys slipped and stumbled on their raw, frozen feet. John Paul got hold of some canvas to make trousers, but he had no way of cutting and sewing them, and it was confiscated.

The *Arran*, as confirmed by the ship's cook, was amply provisioned for its calculated four month return voyage, and the captain at first authorised a fair measure of rations for the stowaways: 5lbs of beef per day, and 14oz of coffee, 7oz of tea and 5lbs of sugar per week. This robust diet shows that the captain began with good intentions. The first thing that went wrong was that the boys succumbed to seasickness, and the mate began to grumble as he saw them vomiting up the chunks of precious beef. He ordered the steward to stop all supply of the beef to them, saying that he was going to give them the ground of their stomachs before they got any more meat. From now on, only the notorious ship biscuits were to be issued to them. That meant one a day, each, if they were in luck. The cook secretly passed them scraps because they were nearing starvation level.

Weakened, the boys, especially the little ones, could scarcely perform their allotted tasks and the mate came after them with a rope's end to give them a walloping. James Bryson, the unfortunate one, further incensed the mate by his dirty habits. One day, when it was fine, the hatches were opened up, and the oakum and coils of rope where the boys slept were found to be 'smeared with filth'. Presumably there was a makeshift latrine. The mate's wrath was concentrated on Bryson and that is how he came to be 'scrubbed and flogged' – a remedial Victorian treatment reminiscent of the 'mopping' accorded to 'lunatics' after a weekend chained to their cribs.

Bryson remembered that the flogging with the lead-line came first. David Brand, who was forced to do some of the scrubbing, remembered that the scrubbing came first. Bryson said, 'The mate flogged me for about three minutes. When I was screaming, the master of the vessel came forward. I was then made to lie down on the deck. Several bucketsful of water were thrown on me. It was salt water. The captain then scrubbed me with a hair broom all over my body. The mate then took the broom up and scrubbed me harder than the captain. After the scrubbing was finished I was made to wash my clothes. I was naked at the time.' David Brand said, 'The weather was very cold, but I do not think that it was freezing. Bryson was very dirty and it was on that account that he was scrubbed. I stopped when I thought he was clean. He was crying out. There were about 30 blows given. The captain was present during the flogging, but said or did nothing. I saw blood on Bryson's back.'

On May 10th, after a stormy crossing, the *Arran*, which for some days had been nosing through packs of floating ice, became temporarily but firmly embedded in an ice-field off St George's Bay, on the west coast of the Island of Newfoundland, after passing through Cabot Strait into the Gulf of St Lawrence. The captain and the mate went down on to the thick ice for a walk, to stretch their legs, and while they were away, the two 16-year-olds, Brand and Bryson, dared to go below and scavenge for food. As usual, it was James Bryson who got into trouble.

'I took some currants out of a keg,' he said, 'because I could get nothing else. I was hungry at the time. I took about a fistful of currants and returned to my work of scraping the deck. The mate was coming up the vessel's side when he saw me coming out of the cabin. He ordered my hands to be tied, and Brand and I were searched. Nothing was found on Brand. My pocket was cut on the outside and the currants "kepped" in a saucer. The captain ordered the currants to be given to the other boys. I was afterwards stripped naked by order of the mate. The captain was present all the time and saw what took place. The mate placed my head on the deck, seized my legs, and held them up to his breast while the captain flogged me. He gave me 15 to 20 lashes. I was ordered by the mate to help the boy Currie to scrub the deck when I was stark naked...my semmit was returned to me. *I was then placed on the hatch and the mate told me to tell him all that I had done in my life.*'

The last sentence of Bryson's complaint, although not

altogether clear, does have an uncomfortable feeling to it, as if the mate were deriving some illicit satisfaction. From now on, the mate withdraws from his role as Chief Torturer, and the captain takes over with a new plan for getting rid of his stowaways. They were to be driven down on to the ice, given one biscuit apiece, and told to walk to the shore. No line of land was visible to the naked eye, but the captain assured the boys that through his spyglass he could see houses with people living in them. The distance between the *Arran* and landfall was variously estimated by the crew as from eight to 20 miles. The mate put it at five miles, but he would say that, wouldn't he? In the alternative, the captain suggested, they could, if they preferred, make for another ship, the *Myrtle*, which was also lying fast in the ice one or two miles away from the *Arran*. There were not enough provisions left to feed the boys as well as the crew for the remaining part of the voyage to Quebec, he explained.

Some of the boys had had pieces of biscuit for breakfast. Only two of them went willingly: Reilly, the young man, because he had not given up his dream of finding a job ashore, and Bryson, lately tortured, because he felt that nothing could be worse than what he had already suffered on board. Peter Currie, the favoured one, was allowed to stay. That left four. David Brand, the 16-year-old, refused to go over the side, and the captain caught him by the collar and forced him. Three small boys aged 11 remained.

Hugh McGinnes asked the captain how he could walk on the ice with his bare feet, and the captain said that it would be as well for him to die on the ice as in the ship, as he would get no more food there. John Paul hid himself in the forecastle. The captain went in and brought him out. He went crying to the mate, and the mate said that he would have nothing to do with putting them on the ice. The captain told him to go forward, and struck him with a belaying-pin because he would not leave the rails. John Paul had no shoes either. He had a blue coat. Hugh

McEwan, the boy who had tuberculosis, was hiding in the galley. He began to cry and the captain found him. He had boots and was better clad than any of them. John Paul was crying that his fingers were hurting in the cold and all three little boys were crying as they were made to slide down a rope and stood on the bitter ice, looking up and pleading for food. Several biscuits were thrown down for them and there was a scramble. It was each boy for himself: they were all too weak for acts of conspicuous heroism.

One young man, two youths, and three boys set out on their 12-hour journey. It was between 8.00 and 9.00am and clear daylight. At first they followed the line of the stern of the *Arran*, because the captain had told them that it would lead them to the *Myrtle*, but they could not see her, never saw her all day, and changed their course while still within sight of the *Arran*. They could see a black haze which looked like land. It would be unrealistic to imagine the ice-field as smooth like a rink: it was rutted and humped and progress was slow. They kept together in a small, tattered party. After about 10 or 11 miles, with the shore clearly in sight, conditions worsened and became very dangerous. Until then, the ice had held up well, but now it was beginning to soften and crack, with crevices and separate floes. Sometimes they fell into the icy water and their thin clothes froze on their backs. It is better not to think about their bare feet.

At around midday, the weakest member, Hugh McEwan fell in three times. The first time, James Bryson, the despised one, managed to pull him out, the second time, he scrambled out on his own, but the third time, the ice closed over his face and he was lost. Two of the smallest boys were left. Some hours later, about five miles from the shore, Hugh McGinnes, whose bare feet were swollen, sat down and said he could go no further. They had to leave him. For a good ten minutes as they struggled on, they could hear him 'greeting'. He could not have lasted long: his skin showed through his ragged trousers. On they went, the depleted band of four, one young man, two youths and one small boy, John Paul, who, although barefooted, must have had some extra powers of endurance. Later he said that he had run away to sea for a pleasure sail! He was comfortable at home. He lived with his mother but did not tell her that he was going. He chose the *Arran* because she was a good ship. He did not know the captain.

The long day passed and they reached the rim of the ice-field. One mile of deep, open water lay between them and the houses on the shore-line. Reilly, Bryson and Brand had, surprisingly, been allowed to bring with them some pieces of wood and a batten from the ship, and they tried to ferry across on separate floats of ice, using the wood as paddles. John Paul, one supposes, stood and watched. Just then, a woman looking out to sea saw them, and a boat was sent over to rescue them, as the sun was going down.

Three of the boys never left the safety of St George's Bay until it was time to go home. When he was strong enough, the fourth, Bernard Reilly, made his way southwards to Halifax, Nova Scotia, to seek work. Meanwhile, the ice had creaked loose and released the *Arran*, set free to sail across the gulf of St Lawrence and up the St Lawrence River to Quebec. From harbour there, a member of the crew who could not get the hellish incidents out of his mind, wrote a graphic letter on June 10th to his people in Greenock: 'The boys were thinly clad, and were not able to stand the severe cold. The men could hardly stand it, let alone them...' His account was received with horror by the relatives of the missing boys and a hostile crowd was waiting on the quay when the *Arran* came up the Clyde on July 30th. A boarding party would have attacked the two officers, who locked themselves in the cabin. The police were called to the disturbance, a near riot, but the crowd did not disperse for many hours.

Worse violence might have occurred if it had then been known that two of the children put out on the ice had in fact been lost. The writer of the letter from Quebec did not know. Nor did the captain and the mate. Next day, those two were arrested, taken before the Sheriff and charged with assault. Both were committed for trial and bail was refused. As a part of his enquiries, the procurator fiscal had telegraphed to the police force at St John's, the capital of Newfoundland, and report was now received that two stowaways had died. The prisoners were further charged with murder.

The trial was held back until Brand, Bryson and Paul were brought from Newfoundland and were fit to give evidence. They were taken first in a schooner to St John's on the far eastern coast of the island, and there transferred to the brigantine *Hannah and Bennie*, which was the property of the Provost of Greenock. Home they came on October 1st, well-fed and clothed, to face their new ordeal of a solemn trial in the High Court of Justiciary at Edinburgh, which occupied three days from November 23rd, 1868. Both captain and mate were now charged and indicted with assault and culpable homicide (manslaughter) not murder, and both relied upon a straight denial. Their declarations read out in court were plainly outrageous humbug. The captain swore that he 'invited' the boys to leave the ship and have a 'run' on the ice. 'I pointed out to them houses on the shore, and said to them they might have a fine run ashore.' He denied forcing them to leave but did admit that he 'of course, told them to go'. The mate, against all the very strong evidence, denied the scrubbing and flogging of James Bryson, or that he had compelled the stowaways to leave the ship.

The three survivors present gave corroborative accounts of the cruel sequence, and members of the crew examined for the Crown found themselves strongly criticised for not interceding. Said one George Henry, 'I had no right to interfere with my master and mate: I was a servant.' But, asked a juryman, 'If the master or mate had been going to murder the boys would you have interfered?' The reply was oblique: 'There was a chance of their reaching the shore, and some of them did reach it.' In those violent times, when an officer would fell a crewman with a blow and think nothing of it, or clap him in irons on suspicion of mutiny, the plight of those who watched is understandable.

In the comparable *Martha and Jane* case of 1857, ten years earlier, Captain Henry Rogers, a native of Aberdeen, had inflicted terrible tortures on a seaman named Andrew Rose, who was a 'little weak in the head'. During the voyage from Barbados to Liverpool, the first and the second mate contributed to the unmistakable acts of sadism. Some of the crew gave Rose a little pea-soup and some water when he was crammed into a water-cask for 12 hours, with only the bunghole for ventilation, but one of the mates found out and reacted with so much rage that they dared not to interfere again. Andrew Rose did die, and his three tormentors, found guilty of murder, were sentenced to death. The captain hanged but the mates were reprieved. There is little doubt here that, short of mutiny, the crew were powerless to help.

For the defence, they put up 12-year-old Peter Currie, the boy who had been spared, and he contributed the unlikely information that he heard the mate say that he would wager any man on board £20 the boys would be back to their dinner! The *Arran's* steward, and the boatswain, both indicated that the captain was a kind, quiet man, who rarely interfered with the discipline of the ship. One of them did allow that he thought it was possible for a man to reach the land over the ice, but not for boys so clad. It had not been his place to question the captain. Then two strong witnesses were called as to character. The chaplain of the Seaman's Friend Society, Greenock, said that Captain Watt was so well disposed to boys that it was generally believed that they liked to stow away with him on that account! This seems a preposterous proposition, but we may receive the evidence of the parish minister of Ardrossan and four of his parishioners as to the probity of the captain with less scepticism.

In the famous case of the mutiny on the *Veronica* (1902),

Captain Shaw, who was murdered by the mutineers, was a hard man to serve under, but regarded as quiet and inoffensive among his equals ashore. The editors of the *Notable British Trials* volume on the case, Professor Keeton and John Cameron, remark that 'The two estimates of Captain Shaw are not necessarily contradictory.' No character witnesses are recorded in the aid of the mate of the *Arran*, and, giving up, he changed his plea to guilty of assault, at the close of the evidence for the defence, whereupon the Solicitor-General withdrew the charge of culpable homicide against him. (All knew that he had stood back from forcing the boys who were unwilling over the rails, but who knows who first conceived the plan as captain and mate walked on the ice?)

George Young, for the defence, objected to the pomposity of the Crown's address. His own spirited points grate and jar, even if they lack barristerial pomposity: it was obvious, he said, that the boys belonged to the very worst class, and although not all guilty of theft on board, they did at any rate force the master to provide them with food which was not intended for their consumption. It could hardly be expected that they should be sumptuously fed. Neither was it reasonable to suppose that a merchant vessel would be equipped with spare clothing for the use of stowaway boys. The washing of the dirty lad, Bryson, was not done with a gentle hand, as on an infant, but as a remedial lesson. The flogging had not injured him.

Coming now, as a late argument, and against the substance of the prisoners' previous declarations, to the serious charge, Counsel put it to the jury that, a few days before they left for good, the boys had been put on the ice to give them a fright, and were taken on board again. Reilly and Bryson seemed to have entered into an agreement to try the ice (true) and *asked the smaller boys to join them*. The captain realised that the attempt was fraught with some danger, and although he permitted and probably pressed the little boys to go along with the bigger ones, he was at the same time under the impression that they would return as soon as they saw the perils. (Yet he did not send out a search party, nor did he ever make any enquiries as to their fate.) He did *not* drag the boys from the ship. Anyway, Counsel continued sickeningly, there was no reliable evidence as to death. It would surprise no-one if both McEwan and McGinnes were to turn up alive and well.

In his summing-up, however, the Lord Justice-Clerk was satisfied that the children *were* compelled to leave the *Arran* by threats and force. A very small show of compulsion on the part of a man in authority was sufficient to make them do things against their will. The captain had said that they had better die on the ice than on board the ship. The verdict was that the captain was guilty of culpable homicide, but not of assault. On account of his previous good character, the jury recommended him to the leniency of the Court. The captain was sentenced to 18 months' imprisonment, and the mate to four months'. Loud hisses greeted this astonishing result. We shall name the judge: it was George Patton, who sat only from 1867 to 1869.

Captain and mate served their time, and returned to sea. Captain Watt was said to have died within a year or two, at Pensacola, Florida, which port, incidentally, supplied the sailors responsible for the brutal *Veronica* mutiny. Mate Kerr lived long. Peter Currie died of consumption at the age of 14. James Bryson emigrated with his father and family to America, where James worked as a streetcar conductor. John Paul, the toughest little boy, became a foreman riveter and died in due course at Itchen, Southampton. David Brand was the most successful: he emigrated to Townsville, North Queensland and founded the engineering firm of Brand, Dryborough and Burns. But once you have heard the story, it is very difficult to forget the two boys who did not survive, pushed out on to the ice by a captain reckless as to whether they lived or died.

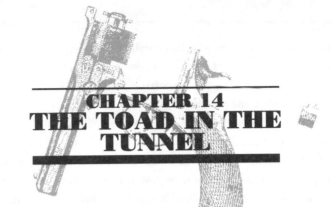

CHAPTER 14
THE TOAD IN THE TUNNEL

T he tradename for the Garvie case, south of the Border at least, is a 'cut-throat' trial, in which co-accused require separate counsel, because each blames the other. This case of 1968, with its three accused, is a study in victimology. Maxwell Robert Garvie, the murdered husband, was the primal victim. He was also, along a chain of causation, the victim of his own lusts, and, disputably, of the age in which he lived – the swinging 60s – whose values he invoked to excuse his bad behaviour. Sheila Garvie, his wife, was a victim of Max Garvie's cruelty, and her own victim. Brian Gordon Tevendale, her lover, convicted with her of the murder, had been drawn into Garvie's perversions and to that extent was the older man's victim. Alan Peters, found Not Proven, was Tevendale's henchman in the disposal of the body, and was under the influence of Tevendale. Peters was probably afraid of him, as he claimed, if only at the material time, and was Tevendale's victim.

Strong women's issues are attached to the case of Sheila Garvie. Her upbringing was repressive, and there was rebellion in her nature. Her father, a sober stonemason, was puritanical and bad-tempered. He was employed on the royal estates at Balmoral and Sheila was placed there in the castle as a domestic servant. Seeing no brightness in life, she escaped to office work and at a dance caught the eye of Max Garvie, a Young Farmer, her social superior who farmed at 'West Cairnbeg', in the Kincardineshire Mearns. On June 11th, 1955 they married. He was 21 and she was 18. In marrying, she moved into another kind of domestic servitude – that of a hostess to farming friends, required to put on bigger and better 'spreads'. In their sexual relationship he cared only for his own gratification and called her frigid. Three children were born, two girls, and in 1964, a son.

Sheila had done well but she was not happy. Garvie was unpredictable and suffered from chronic boredom – not a philosophical ennui, but an immature need to spark off the moment to die now and live later. The action man part of him took to flying; he founded a club and flew his own German-built Bolkow Junior. He enjoyed buzzing cars and boats in true Hitchcock-fashion. Connubial missionary-style sex bored him. One thing led to another. He turned to erotic photography, forced nudism on his unwilling wife and tried to involve their young daughters. The naturists' club that he set up was said to have been called 'Kinky Cottage' by local residents. Very conscious that he was living in the permissive society (he said as much), he moved on to 'wife-swapping' and 'orgies', and encouraged Brian Tevendale, the 22-year-old son of a former Army Provost for Scottish Command, to pay attention to Sheila. Trudy Birse, Tevendale's sister and married to Alfred Birse, a policeman, was for Max Garvie.

At least twice, Garvie was violent towards Sheila. Once he threatened to shoot her. She was afraid of him. Although Trudy pleased him more than Sheila, he remained a possessive husband with a dominant personality. Sheila found his sexual demands of her disgusting and perverted. He seems to have been a polymorphous pervert! Reading between the lines, for she would never say, he was of Mellors' inclination – a fair reference since the *Lady Chatterley* trial was fresh in people's minds and was to pop up at the Garvie trial. Sheila began to suffer from depression quite early in the marriage. He drank heavily, always looking for stimulation, downing perhaps five bottles of whisky a week and taking 'handfuls' of Pro-Plus (a caffeine compound still on sale over the counter today), especially as an aid to flying, together with the addictive sleeping-pill, Soneryl, a butobarbitone. We can only imagine the drugs to which he would have been drawn in the 1990s – Ecstasy, no doubt, would have been at the top of his list.

All this time, Max Garvie kept on farming well enough with the help of a grieve, although Sheila complained that farming magazines went straight into the wastepaper-basket, unlike the stream of pornographic magazines. He was a man obsessed. It was useless for fringe friends, business associates, fellow-flyers to deny the other side of the Young Farmer, because, although lies were to fly in the court of trial, Sheila Garvie's own mother, Mrs Edith Watson, a painfully upright woman, knew all about it and testified so. She was the last person in the world to lie about the state of her daughter's marriage, since, as we shall see, she was the one who exposed the murder.

Then Sheila and Brian Tevendale discovered that they loved each other. It became an increasingly disintegrative picture, with scenes, departures and returns. Garvie was impossible to cope with. He threatened to put her away in a clinic in London. It is a sad aspect of the case that the abused wife appealed for help from her mother, a solicitor, a clergyman, and a hotelier who became involved, but they all urged her to stick with her husband for the sake of the children. So far, this morality tale of the sixties sounds like the setting for a wife-murder, but Max Garvie it was who disappeared. He was last seen alive on the evening of May 14th 1968, heading homewards.

Officially, he was a missing man. Sheila and Tevendale were spotted around together, enjoying each other's company. Sheila's mother disapproved and on August 14 she went to the police in some agony of mind and physical collapse to inform them that Sheila had indicated to her that Garvie was dead and had not died naturally. She said that Brian Tevendale was 'a strong man at her back'. Sheila had obviously not known where the body was to be disposed of, because she had asked her mother about the seatides, when, as soon emerged, Tevendale (helped by Peters) had had a different inspiration for concealment of the body.

Sheila Garvie and Tevendale were arrested on that same day, and Alan Peters somewhat later. Quite soon, Tevendale led the police to an underground tunnel or culvert running from Lauriston Quarry to the west side of Lauriston Castle, near the village of St Cyrus. Along that tunnel the police saw by torchlight a pile of stones on which a large toad was squatting. There is an old folklore belief that a toad hopping over your foot is a presage of death. Underneath this subterranean cairn, they found the body of Max Garvie, the 'flying farmer', grounded now for ever. There was a gunshot wound of the neck and the skull was fractured.

Tevendale's statement to the police spared Alan Peters, whom he did not mention, but blamed Sheila, although only to the extent of a most extraordinary accident. His version, which was not believed, was that Sheila had called him to come down to the farmhouse. He found her in a terrible state, saying that her husband had died accidentally. He had required her to do something unnatural with a rifle. She had refused, there had been a struggle, and the gun had gone off. He, Tevendale, had disposed of the body for her.

Alan Peters' statement implicated Tevendale and Sheila Garvie and set out a premeditated murder at which he himself was present but passive. He had helped with the removal and concealment of the body – this was never disputed. Several weeks previously, Peters said, Tevendale had brought it up that he wanted to get rid of the bloke and asked him if he would come with him to provide transport. On the night, they parked on the road at the back of 'West Cairnbeg', went from there into the garage and '*Mrs Garvie let us into the house*'. Tevendale got the gun from the back of the door and they went through into the sitting-room. Mrs Garvie gave them a drink and then she showed them to a room upstairs. They waited until Mr Garvie came home and went to bed and when he was asleep Mrs Garvie came through and told them. Then they (and from the context he seems to mean only the two men) went through and Tevendale hit Mr Garvie on the head with the butt of the gun and then shot him.

Sheila Garvie's version of this brutal bedside murder placed the two men in the murder room and distanced herself from the murder, with some good circumstantial detail. She was woken, she said, some time after 11.30pm, by someone whispering to her to get up. The bedroom light was off but the room was lit from the landing light. She recognised the voice and figure as being those of Brian Tevendale. He took her by the arm out on to the landing and there was another man standing there, a fair-haired man whom she did not know at all. She was hustled into the bathroom and told to get in and stay there. She noticed that 'he' (not specified) was carrying a gun. She did not know at that time that it belonged to her husband. She heard the bedroom door closing, and 'terrible thumping noises'.

After about five minutes, Tevendale tried the bathroom door. She unlocked it. He said something like 'You won't have any more of him to put up with.' He asked her to stay beside the girls' door in case they came out. After a while the two men pulled her husband from the bedroom in a sort of groundsheet.

All three were brought up for trial at the High Court in Aberdeen on November 19th 1968 and they all pleaded Not Guilty. It was a sensational murder trial by reason of the sexual revelations, and it was much enjoyed by those who had never felt a wound. It was noticed that the older generation particularly relished the spectacle of the downfall of younger members of society who had enjoyed a freedom denied to them, and who had come to a sticky end.

Yet there was intense human misery attached to the proceedings: one woman juror was so affected by the distress of Sheila Garvie's mother that she fainted and the trial continued with only fourteen in the jury box. At one stage, Max Garvie's skull was produced in court from a cardboard box, and held aloft with riveting effect.

Brian Tevendale, unlike his two co-accused, did not give evidence on his own behalf, and he was to be found guilty by unanimous verdict. Sheila Garvie appeared weak and tired, and the case raises questions about evidence given by a person so 'tranquillised' by Valium or Librium, new drugs then, that she felt depersonalised, out of herself, with her mouth and throat dry and painful after hours in the witness-box. It must be said, even so, that her evidence as reported was very able and consistent. Would the jury have believed her if she had not dyed her dark hair blonde? Ruth Ellis, convicted of murder in 1955, had also been seen as a 'brassy blonde'.

Contemporary commentators at the Garvie trial did not think that her tales of her husband's cruelty brought her much sympathy. The predicament of the trapped wife was not greatly understood. If she were guilty, as she was found, it was a clever bluff for a woman of her limited background to insist that 'I felt morally responsible because I had allowed Brian to fall in love with me and had become emotionally involved with him. I felt I had unconsciously provoked him in the emotional state in which he was. I was at a crossroads in my life. I took a decision that night that, whatever happened, I would protect Brian because of what he had done for me.'

Under Scottish law, those defending her had lodged a pre-trial notice of intent to attack the character of the dead man. As Laurence Dowdall, her solicitor, later commented, this was a two-edged sword because it provided a motive for murder. In fact, it looked more like a lead-up to a defence of provocation! The background would probably have come out in the course of the proceedings, anyway. The 'attack' on Max Garvie was to explain the whole constellation of circumstances and to stand against any idea that this was an ordinary eternal triangle and a conspiracy to murder an unwanted husband, retain her standard of living, cash-in insurances, and keep the children.

Although Sheila tried to explain that the three doomed last months of freedom with Tevendale after the murder were a nightmare of guilt and terror, this final period must have alienated the jury, especially when a picnic photograph was produced, in which another man was light-heartedly lying on top of her.

The crunch or turning-point of the trial from Sheila Garvie's point of view was a section of Trudy Birse's evidence which was unexpected and certainly did not come up to proof. Trudy, described as a green-eyed feline extravert was, it will be remembered, Max Garvie's girlfriend, one member of his orchestrated quartet, and she was also a Crown witness. Even so, under the Scottish system of law, Laurence Dowdall was able to interview her before trial – it was quite permissible – and he had not found her hostile to his client. In his 'Postscript' to Sheila Garvie's own story, entitled *Marriage to Murder* (Chambers, 1980) Laurence Dowdall describes his shock when, in court, she departed from her previous account and damaged his client. Let us use the words of the trial judge, Lord Thomson, on this point:

> *There is in the evidence a good deal of doubt as to how much Mrs Garvie said to Mrs Birse after the murder and how much Tevendale said to Mrs Birse and how much was said when both Sheila Garvie and Tevendale were present. If you accept Mrs Birse's evidence there is evidence that Mrs Garvie said to Mrs Birse something to the effect that she had gone into the room upstairs and told Tevendale and Peters that Max was asleep. If that is true, it is a damning piece of evidence against her.*

Both solicitor and advocate for Sheila Garvie thought that Trudy Birse had been under emotional strain, that she was not a liar, and not a malicious woman. Laurence Dowdall thought that she really did not know what she was saying, and that she was the greatest enigma in the case.

A point in Sheila Garvie's defence, upon which she placed much confidence, was her ability to disprove the damning part of Alan Peters' statement in which he said that she 'let them in' from the garage to the farmhouse. The plain meaning of the phrase, presumably, is that without her intercession, they *could* not have gained access. She said, and her mother confirmed this, that there was no lock on the connecting door, and a joiner was brought to testify that he had fitted a lock to the door in question at a date *after* the murder. By the time of his actual evidence in court, however, Alan Peters had modulated his previous statement: they went in through the garage and at the end of a corridor leading from the garage into the house they were met by Mrs Garvie. He was unable to say whether or not she was expecting them but she did not seem surprised that they were there.

Peters, who was only 20 years old, stood up well to cross-examination and he must have struck a chord with the jury when he said that he was afraid that 'If I didn't assist [Tevendale] in any way I would get the same'. On those lines, his lawyers had lodged the unusual special defence of coercion by Brian Tevendale. The judge, however, in his summing-up, directed the jury that coercion was simply not open to Peters and that they must disregard it. It had never anyway been decided in Scotland whether coercion could ever be a defence to a charge of murder. Even so, (Lord Thomson told the jury) Peters' state of mind was still relevant.

Sheila Garvie had the advantage of a spectacular defence team – Laurence Dowdall had briefed Lionel Daiches, QC – and it was clearly a shock and a disappointment to them when they did not secure an acquittal, although the adverse verdict was only by a majority. Her solicitor suggested that if the jury had had the opportunity to consider their verdict on the same day as silver-tongued Lionel Daiches had addressed them, they would have acquitted, but a weekend lay between his speech on a Friday and the judge's charge on the following Monday. We might wonder about that. Mr Daiches' peroration took the form of quotation of the famous passage from John Donne's *Meditations* (the first part of *Devotions upon Emergent Occasions*) – 'No man is an island entire of itself; every man is a piece of the Continent, a part of the main... Any man's death diminishes me, because I am involved in mankind; and therefore never send to know for whom the bell tolls; it tolls for thee...' 'And', modern Counsel ended, 'for all of us.'

In old murder trials it was fully expected of flamboyant defence counsel that there would be appeals to the Bard and snippets from the Classics. William Roughead effortlessly filled his essays with references to Stevenson, Shakespeare, Webster, Galt, Scott, Dickens and Conrad... This seems to be perfectly acceptable as long as the quotation springs naturally to the mind, and Donne was all the rage in the 1960s, with the 'no man is an island' sentiment widely subsumed in thoughts about 'commitment'. Even if the man on the Clapham omnibus was not privy to the whole text, he certainly knew his filmed Hemingway. However, a discerning Scottish jury might not have appreciated the incongruous connection between so fine a piece of literature and a particularly sordid criminal case, nor the implication that, given a moved notch or two in their circumstances, they would have found themselves in Sheila Garvie's shoes.

After ten years in prison, Sheila Garvie was released on parole in September, 1978, and published her book in 1980. Brian Tevendale was released three months later, in December. He was reported as making certain colourful remarks which implicated Sheila Garvie in the actual commission of the crime, but what he said then was not evidence and would be out of place in a book of this nature. Sheila quickly remarried. She had taken over from her aunt and uncle a boarding-house in Aberdeen, and there she met a young Rhodesian, David McLellan. After only eight months, the union ended in 'violence

and bitterness'. She had made another wrong choice. On Christmas Eve, 1981, she married again: her third husband was Charles Burdon Mitchell, a drilling engineer.

CHAPTER 15
BIBLE JOHN

Serial killers should, perhaps, be assigned to a new subcategory of insanity. 'Sadistic sexual psychopath' is beginning to seem no longer an adequate diagnosis for the incorrigible desire to kill other human beings. The categories of madness are not necessarily closed. If we could look the killer firmly in the eye and say, 'You think that it is all right to carry on killing, and therefore you are insane. You are suffering from Serial Killer Psychosis [or whatever] and you must stay locked up because there is no cure for your condition', then we have cleared the air, and the issue has not been fudged. The offender knows how he stands and how he is viewed by society.

A serial killer is totally consumed by his intention to kill and kill again. He is not curable. He is not amenable to reason. Remorse is lacking. He is like an alien, programmed with a different agenda from the rest of us. That is why studies like that headed by Andrian Raine of the University of California (v. *Daily Telegraph*, 14th April 1998) may ultimately be of more value than the art of 'psychological profiling'. Raine found that a study of 38 murderers indicated that it was possible to be born without a part of the brain involved in creating 'a sense of conscience'. He described an 'identifiable biological dysfunction'.

It is now official that some score or so serial killers walk among us on this island. The lay person instinctively feels that this tribe of outcasts 'must be mad' and is puzzled and disappointed by the routine label. It might be thought that if we account them mad, then the concept that they are 'evil' is no longer available. We are somehow reluctant to offer them the 'excuse' of actual mental illness, of not being able to help themselves. This, however, is what we should recognise, because it means that we acknowledge the dangerous inflexibility of the condition, a madness in its own right, standing with the major psychoses and defined with its own observed symptomatology.

Some serial killers do develop the symptoms of schizophrenia, anyway. Unless everything that he stated or let slip during one whole evening at the Barrowland Ballroom in Glasgow ,on October 30th 1969, was deliberately calculated to mislead, Bible John's conversation and behaviour as he prepared the ground for his third known murder of a young woman was in fact quite abnormal and paranoid in character, so much so that it might have been noticed if he had been in some structured setting, as was widely thought, such as the military or the police. It is possible, but it does not seem very likely, that he was clever and cool enough to plan or improvise a number of clued remarks which he seeded into the conversation with his victim, Helen Puttock, and her observant sister, Jeannie Williams, such as, 'My father says these places are dens of iniquity. They set fire to this place to get the insurance money, and done it up with the money.' He prated of 'adulterous women' and disapproved of married women frequenting the Barrowland. When asked what he did at the New Year, he said that he did not drink, but prayed. He was an agnostic, though (an inconsistency of sorts) and did not believe in all that religious carry-on.

The abnormal and inappropriate behaviour occurred when he overreacted and made a scene about a faulty cigarette machine, ranting, asking for the manager, and enquiring who the MP for the area was. (But he showed local geographical knowledge and knew the logistics of getting around Glasgow without a car...) It is a strange thought that he might have knowingly constructed a pious characterisation for himself, and later rejoiced at his given title, Bible John, while the real man behind the mask was *nothing like* his invention. Jeannie Williams in the taxi with the unobservant driver which bore them away from the Barrowland late at night, saw glimpses of the real man, no longer polite and correct but cold, angry, silent and arrogant.

Can we, then, see Bible John as he really was, perhaps cleverly inventive of his false persona, strutting about his small back bedroom or obscure bedsitter gloating over his newspaper coverage, his shabby bookcase bursting with the obligatory mental furniture of the serial killer – Nazism, the occult, sado-masochism, true crime, and so on – and organised in pride of place his Barrowland trophies, a handbag and some clothing spirited away from his pleasurable outings? But we must not mock him because he *is* mad. He carries within his lonely mind the consuming drive to kill – Serial Killer Psychosis in itself – or he is already germinating, or in the throes of, a good old-fashioned schizophrenia, in which latter case, he has been unable to prevent Jeannie Williams from glimpsing the seething delusions and disordered religious thoughts which torment him. Additionally, SKP may merge into schizophrenia during the sequence of the crimes, as appeared to be happening to Ted Bundy in America and to the Yorkshire Ripper, now in Broadmoor.

There must be a significance in Bible John's choice of the Barrowland as the place to find his victims. He may simply have felt at home there, not uncomfortable. The very name may have meant something personal to him, such as an image of a wasteland with someone – him, watching himself – trundling a barrow containing a body. His thought content may have been rich and bizarre. The futuristic, bleak, 1930s façade, like some gateway to an imagined Science Fiction Hell, might have attracted him. Or he may simply have thought it more louche than other halls such as the Majestic, especially on Thursday nights for the over-25s, when he knew as well as anyone that married women without their wedding-rings and married men all calling themselves 'John' made their way to the Barrowland for illicit encounters.

Inveigh as he might against adulterous women, it was precisely on a Thursday night that he made two of his catches. Patricia Docker, aged 25, was in fact separated, a nursing auxiliary at Mearnskirk Hospital, and she went to the dancing on Thursday, February 22nd 1968. Helen Puttock, aged 29, was certainly married, and she left her husband baby-sitting when she went with her sister to the Barrowland on Thursday October 30th 1969. The victim in the middle, Jemima Mcdonald, aged 32, was a single mother of three children, and she did go to the Thursday nights, but actually encountered Bible John on Saturday night, August 16th 1969.

All three young women, brunettes, dressed in the 60s finery of short dresses, with elaborate make-up and hairstyles, were described as vivacious and attractive, but, meaning no unkindness, they did not have film-star good looks and Bible John steered clear of conspicuous blonde bombshells. Presenting himself as of NCO-type, with pinned-on inappropriate good manners, such as pulling out a chair for his dancing partner as if they were at a tea-dance and not a whirling, jiving, bacchic scene, he was (to use an anachronism) a toff to them, and an exciting catch. They were not prostitutes, but ordinary Glasgow girls leading hard lives, just getting by, full of spirit.

Bible John could easily have picked up prostitutes on the streets or in the bars if that had been his fancy, but he was not like Jack the Ripper with a 'down on whores', although we have a right to postulate that he did not like women. He did not seem to be a married man and he never, incidentally, mentioned a mother during his personal revelations although there seemed to be a sister, which detail he retracted. Perhaps he avoided prostitutes because, unlike Jack the Ripper, he was intent on full sexual congress. His design was rape, if necessary, followed by strangulation with a ligature such as the victim's tights or one of her stockings. There was something about the lively, flirtatious girls dancing their cares away at the Barrowland that appealed to him, and he went back for more.

On how many occasions, not always successful, he prowled the ballroom, leaning nonchalantly against a pillar and watching the action, we simply do not know. With his now famous red or sandy hair, cut unfashionably short, especially for a man of his age – somewhere between 25 and 35 – together with a decent suit and half-boots so unfashionable that passing 'hard lads' twitted him as he left with his prey on his arm, he was reckless that he stood out from the crowd and quite confident that his semi-professional style would secure a compliant girl. The *modus operandi* was politely to escort her nearly to her home, a guardian in such dangerous times, and then lure her or persuade her to invite him to a nearby dark corner for some sexual favours. Screams were heard only once.

It is a very curious fact that all three victims were menstruating at the time when they were killed. To a woman, that seems extra cruel, but that concept would have no reality to Bible John in his madness. It is difficult not to equate his expressed opinions on women with the Mosaic law (Leviticus 15.19) that a menstruating woman is 'unclean'. Bible John did not 'preach' at the two girls in the taxi, nor 'spout' long extracts from the Bible, but as he mumbled evasively while trying to preserve a front of normality, he did show familiarity with the text of the Bible. In particular he seemed to refer to a woman being stoned, and to Moses in the bulrushes, and he seemed to have a preoccupation with childhood deprivation and foster homes.

Sophisticated crime-writers like to say that it was a mere coincidence that all three women were in the same physical condition, but it is one of those things that are not proveable, and common-sense does seem to indicate that it is relevant. It is, however, ridiculous to suggest that Bible John with his feral instincts could sense when that was so. Whether or not a Glasgow girl in the swinging sixties would offer that information when it became obvious that some sexual contact might be in view is a different matter. Not that she would necessarily have rejected his advances for that reason, anyway. It must be a valid possibility that he eliminated them because of their condition – that it was a trigger. By this reasoning, on other occasions he could have satisfied himself without committing any crime and spared the girl. The trouble with this thinking is that reports by women of having safely entertained a man met at the Barrowland who resembled the description provided by Jeannie Williams did not come up.

Nor did another stranger, 'Castlemilk John' emerge from the thickets to help Jeannie Williams with the 300 or so identification parades which she so willingly attended. He had been her dancing partner on that last evening and she thought that he was a married man. They had all made up an impromptu foursome and the two men had ample opportunity for conversation, although he was not in the taxi at the end. He told Jeannie that he was a slater or builder from Castlemilk. We may charitably hope that as he read the newspaper over the family breakfast table he reasoned that he did not have anything substantial to add to the search for Bible John, who vanished as mysteriously as Jack the Ripper. There was supposed to have been a last sighting of him at about 2.00am on the following Friday morning, when a dishevelled man with a dirty jacket and a red mark on his cheek was spotted on a night service bus plying along Dumbarton Road, but it has not been made at all clear why he should have been the one.

No-one could have anything but admiration for the intensity and dedication of the investigation under Detective Superintendent Joe Beattie. It is impossible to think of a clue – and there were many promising leads – which he did not pursue to infinity. As in the case of the Yorkshire Ripper, it is now thought that the team was overwhelmed by the cumbersome card-indexes and files which were to be superseded by computer technology. If Bible John had been so disordered in his mind that he had continued to frequent the Barrowland, where it was joked that the police had a formation dance team on the floor, of course he would have been caught. Other unsolved murders in Scotland which followed in 1977 were mooted, but with not much conviction, as his handiwork. Since, notionally, the Barrowland was a vital feature of his insanity and, unhindered, he would have carried on with his work into double figures, it might be that when he was, as it were, locked out of the core of his fantasy, the impulse died. Perhaps.

Because Joe Beattie did not succeed, he was criticised for relying so heavily on his chief eye-witness but there is no doubt that Jeannie Williams had scrutinised Helen's partner as closely as if she had almost had a premonition. (And she certainly felt misgivings in the taxi when he was morose and clearly could not wait to get rid of her.) There was the promising matter of his dentition. She observed that his two (middle?) front teeth overlapped slightly and that one tooth, number 4 or 5 in dental terms, was missing on the right upper jaw. Several hundred Glasgow dentists were circulated and over 5,300 men thrown up by this enquiry were interviewed and eliminated. Perhaps a young man with such a gap in his teeth had not been to the dentist for some time, although someone must have extracted the missing tooth. Serial killers do not like being hurt.

The red or sandy hair cut quite short and rounded at the back seemed like a gift at first and Glasgow hairdressers and barbers – some 450 of them – were questioned in vain. If Bible John had been wearing some kind of false hair, one feels that Jeannie would have spotted it. The author is open to correction, but believes that a man in the 1960s would have had difficulty in obtaining a product which would dye his hair a convincing shade of red or sandy that could be washed out after the dance. It is well known that young men of this hair colouring were collared in the streets by members of the public during the very open investigation. If Bible John chose to stay in Glasgow and lie low, the red hair must have been a problem to him because anyone who knew him, if only the assistant at the corner-shop where he bought staples of food, would immediately have been suspicious if he had suddenly changed his hair colour. For one thing, hair dyeing was much more unusual then than it is now.

Bible John said in the taxi that he worked in a laboratory, knew the public houses in Yoker, and mentioned that he had plenty of money, but all of this material was regarded from the first as a deliberate lie, and none of it helped. His choice of a laboratory as a respectable job is interesting – it is not the first avocation which would occur to most men out to cut a dash. Perhaps he had some bubbling phials of chemicals in his home or digs and experimented with poisons – that would be a typical serial killer's hobby. He was a non-smoker, which helped in a negative way when ticking off points in assessing a suspect. Hundreds of men were eliminated: Jeanie Williams was the final arbiter.

There were some especially tantalising hidden clues in the case. What was the nature of the badge on Bible John's lapel which he kept fingering and putting his thumb over as if he were trying to conceal it from Jeannie and Castlemilk John? It did not matter if Helen Puttock saw it. It appeared that Bible John had not realised that Helen was 'with' Jeannie until it was too late and he had already worked on his prey. The other two victims had been on their own and were happy to leave with him. This may have been the cause of some of his bad behaviour at the cigarette machine and in the taxi before he dropped Jeannie off; he was milling over his mistake and facing up to the fact that this time there were two good eye-witnesses and that his turn at the Barrowland was over. Jeannie just thought that he was angry with her for being in the way. Strangely, she, Jeannie, did not want him to know where she lived, and stopped the taxi accordingly, but Helen was driven on oblivious to her doom. It was after midnight, they were all tired, it was dark in the taxi, whiskies had been taken earlier in the evening at the Trader's Tavern, Helen had made her choice and judgement had gone. There were signs of a deadly struggle and a chase where Helen had tried to climb a railway embankment. Those who knew her said that she would have put up a fight and used her long finger-nails.

The presumably assumed name of Helen's partner, which Jeannie only half heard and did not take in properly – John Templeton or Sempleson or Emerson – might have had some significance. In the cloakroom, Helen told Jeannie some detail about her partner, something about where he lived or worked, but she could not remember what it was although she racked her memory for years. Hypnosis might have been able to retrieve it, but the Crown Office in Edinburgh vetoed the plan which was already in place, with Jeannie willing and Dr Raymond Antebi of Duke Street Hospital, Glasgow, prepared to give it a go.

There was a curious incident just after the scene over the faulty cigarette machine, when Jeannie saw that Helen's John was saying something to her which she did not seem to believe because she was shaking her head (or was it a frank proposition?). Then he produced some card or paper, pink, perhaps, from his pocket, and Helen's attitude changed from a kind of playful incredulity to surprised acceptance. Jeannie tried to get a look at it, but he slipped it back in his pocket, saying, 'You know what happens to nosy folk' and tapping the side of his nose in a vulgar gesture. Like the badge, the nature of the card is anyone's guess but it is the change in Helen's attitude which is telling. All the girls who frequented the Barrowland carried in their minds – but it was fading now – the knowledge that two of their number had been murdered in that and the previous year and to some, limited it seems, extent, they were on their guard.

Neither sister, obviously, recognised any likeness between Helen's partner, as he appeared at the dancing and in the taxi, and the black and white line-drawing prepared after the second murder by an artist, Lennox Paterson, of the Glasgow School of Art, which had been shown on television and reproduced in newspapers. There had been no eye-witnesses to the encounter between Bible John and his first victim, Patricia Docker, but two witnesses had been found in the Jemima McDonald case. A boy thought that he had seen her sitting in a public house with a man, while a girl thought that she had seen her sitting on a sofa in the Barrowland with a man who was good looking, and some of whose features she could describe in the most general sense.

When, however, Jeannie arrived on one of her first visits to the Marine Police Office to be interviewed by Joe Beattie, she saw that first drawing on the wall of the office and said immediately, 'That's like him.' She was taken to see Lennox Paterson and from her impressions he did the famous colour painting, which he later refined, and which was in its turn widely circulated. To the author, this 'portrait' has always had the look of the young John Ruskin, Victorian writer and thinker, and that is strange, because Ruskin, too, had peculiar ideas about women, finding their bodies repellent, and being unable to consummate his marriage. But the face of the killer, refined, as it were, by a freak of nature, is only a mask. The mind inside the 60-year-old (or so) face now, years later, its hair grey or metallic-dyed, still feels no remorse, no desire to confess.

The police should have known that John Irvine McInnes was not the one, when he boasted and laughed in his village of Stonehouse about having been pulled in to identification parades, and was happy to be known locally as Bible John! It is not entirely clear to an outsider why an early suspect eliminated by Joe Beattie, not identified by Jeannie Williams, should have been elevated into a prime suspect in 1995. DS Beattie had retired in 1976, and genetic profiling had been developed in the 1990s. It was thought in the city that a political agenda lay behind the decision to use DNA testing in an attempt to close the Bible John case for all time. If a resounding success could be achieved, then, so the thinking went, a spanking new national DNA databank might be set up at Strathclyde. A stain on Helen Puttock's clothing had been preserved and it was found to yield DNA. We do not know if the stain was the sole such specimen, but that is the implication. There was then a wide logical jump to apply the matching technique to a suspect, for Joe Beattie's investigation had eliminated all those first suspected. The old data was put on computer and the name of McInnes apparently kept coming up, and so a new enquiry concentrated on him, fuelled perhaps by old hunches and suspicions. Jeannie Williams, who had passed him over, when now shown his Scots Guards photograph, pointed out that his 'jug ears' were absolutely wrong. She could not look at him again in the flesh, because he had committed suicide at the age of 41 on April 29th, 1980. Circumstantial evidence included his strict upbringing by parents of the Plymouth Brethren sect, his red hair, and the fact that he was at the Barrowland on the night of the Helen Puttock killing. He had not confessed.

It is understood that two relatives of John McInnes, a brother and a sister, agreed to have samples taken for DNA analysis and that the match with the Bible John stain was sufficiently close for an exhumation of McInnes' body to be sought. Again, the relatives gave permission. Great distress was undoubtedly caused. The grave was opened on February 1st 1996. Unfortunately, the coffin of the mother who had died aged 91 had first to be uplifted. DNA tests referred to Cambridge University and the Institute of Forensic Medicine in Berlin proved negative. Even if the result had been positive, the authorities may not have realised the abhorrence felt by many people of different disciplines. Going on a fishing expedition, disturbing graves, a profound taboo, especially when relatives are still living, seems to be a novel procedure, like cloning, which needs to be watched.

There is a view that it is no worse, and in the interests of science and justice, than the exhumation of a body to determine true cause of death upon suspicion, but the cases are not on equal terms. A murder victim cries out from the grave for justice. If no foul play is discovered, no harm has been done. A suspected husband, say, has been vindicated. A murderer disclosed by DNA in his own grave cannot be convicted. The relatives of his victim are partially satisfied by the revealed truth. It is a moral, not a legal justice. But if the grave of an innocent person is disturbed, there is neither legal nor moral satisfaction. Judging from the precedent of the McInnes disaster, the relatives of the person traduced could feel relief but would have preferred the uncertainty of not knowing. Elimination of multiple suspects dead from suicide or natural causes by sampling from grave to grave would clearly be indefensible.

CHAPTER 16
JOCK THE RIPPER

The compulsion to make false confession, to enjoy a fleeting vainglory, be important, a somebody, the focus of attention, is a little more frightening when attached to a pretendant to Jack the Ripper, because a nasty murder or two will often have preceded the claim.

The most famous Ripper confessor was undoubtedly Dr Thomas Neill Cream, the Lambeth poisoner, who fed strychnine to prostitutes. The legend is that Billington the hangman heard him say, 'I am Jack the ...' just as the bolt was drawn. An obscurer case, on the Continent, is that of a Frenchman named Oulie, who 'called himself Jack the Ripper' and was condemned to penal servitude for life at the Aveyron Assizes in 1889. He had butchered a shrieking woman in her own room, fled, and jumped into a pond with suicidal intent. Fished out by pursuing gendarmes and put up for trial, he argued in his own defence that the dead woman had ruined him physically for life, and therefore he had a right to his revenge. Sometimes the false confessor is insane and suffers from a delusion that he has actually offended as he insists. There is also a type of severe obsessive-compulsive, who wonders, as the notion preys on him, if he *might* have done it. Or there is the unsatisfactory case of the befuddled alcoholic who wonders if *he* might have done it. (As happened to Philip Yale Drew, the actor suspected in 1929 of murdering a tobacconist in Reading.)

William Henry Bury, the Dundee Ripper, self-confessed Jack, was a known alcoholic, but (the author believes) may well have been an *insane* alcoholic. He has become of the colourful company of Jack the Ripper suspects, and there has been many a worse candidate. The dates have to be right (as they are here): i.e. he has to be placed in the Metropolis between (arguably) August and November 1888, and decent propinquity to Whitechapel is persuasive, the more so if the suspect has a reason to be on the streets (as here). However, the method of killing and the nature of the rippings have to be an exact match (as here they are not) for the suspect to be declared of classic cut. Also, funnily enough, the mere fact that someone said he was Jack the Ripper somehow makes it the less likely that he was so.

Not a great deal of material has appeared so far about William Henry Bury, even though there is a piquancy in the concept of Jack removed to Scotland and hanged there, his identity disclaimed by the London Establishment. Euan MacPherson from Montrose announced in the *Sunday Mail* of January 10th 1988, that he believed that Bury was the Ripper, and that he had completed a book to that effect. A photograph of a young-looking Euan in his sweater, in the mode of Colin Wilson at the time of his *The Outsider*, one elbow on a fine pile of manuscript, accompanies the feature. Sadly, the book has never appeared (at this time of writing) although it would be received with great interest. A good entry on Bury was included in the *Scots Black Kalendar* and Donald M Fraser, in *Scottish Mysteries* (Mercat Press, Edinburgh, 1977) has gone to contemporary sources to produce a fresh and detailed account.

Bury was born in Wolverhampton in 1859, that landmark year of the publication of *On the Origin of Species*, but what was Darwin to him? Euan MacPherson, in a taster for his full, promised book, a feature appearing in *The Scots Magazine* (January 1988) revealed the family history which his research had produced. Bury had an elder brother and sister and, most importantly, his mother became insane when Bury was six months old. She died in Worcester County Asylum – that is 'Powick', lately toppled to dust and covered over by estate houses. It was one of the great county asylums, erected out of sheer philanthropism, and sheltered many poor souls, some of whom yet wander the streets as if this were the Middle Ages, and are now less well received than then. The author visited the site in the summer of 1996 and saw the last long hall turned into a shell, the hills of Malvern showing through cavernous gaps in its tenacious structure. There are no details of the mother's illness, nor of the father.

When he was 18 years old, Bury moved to London. In the year of the Ripper, 1888, aged about 29, Bury married, in April, a girl named Ellen Elliott. By then he was already an alcoholic, improvident and violent. Most people imagine Jack the Ripper as a loner, constitutionally wifeless, but the Yorkshire Ripper, Peter William Sutcliffe, is a glaring proof of the exception. Bury's habitat was Bow, a poor, crowded part of the East End, nothing to do with Bow Bells, Cheapside, and Bow Street, Strand. If not quite contiguous to Whitechapel, it lies only a mile or so, depending on your point of reference, to the broad north-east. If you lived there in 1888, both districts probably felt like much the same territory.

It is still possible to find in directories the three known streets in which Bury lived. There may have been more: he was certainly a cheat and a bilker. He lodged with an Elizabeth Haynes in Swaton Road (the first matrimonial home); at 11 Blackthorn Street; and at 3 Spanby Road. All were within a quarter-mile triangle in Bow. Limehouse Cut, a terrifying canal, ran south-west to the docks. Bury was an employed man, although he was only just employable. He worked as a sand and sawdust seller for James Martin, of Bromley, who also employed Ellen Bury, his wife, as a domestic servant. This *cannot* be, as given, Bromley, Kent, a salubrious suburb some ten miles south-west of London, but rather Bromley-by-Bow, with its self-explanatory name. It was in Bow, incidentally, that an earlier bogeyman, Spring Heeled Jack, capered up to Bearbinder Cottage, Bearbinder Lane and assaulted Miss Jane Alsop.

As for Bury's trade, the delivery of sand and sawdust has possibilities. Donald Fraser comments that he would have known the byways of Whitechapel as well as anyone. Euan MacPherson proposes that he could have kept a set of clean clothing in the cart to change into if bloodstained. We may suppose that sand and sawdust were in demand for shovelling over the floors of shops, lodging-houses, public houses, and slaughterhouses – with which Jack the Ripper has often been linked. Neat as it is to imagine Bury as a frequenter of the Whitechapel abattoirs, the reality may be that his horse merely plodded around Bow and Bromley! Sand and sawdust is a heavy load, and a large, slow draught-horse would have been needed to convey it.

The marriage, a fatal choice for Ellen, was doomed from the beginning. Her charm for him was that she had an impressive inheritance of shares left to her by an aunt who had died seven years previously. It took him a couple of months to winkle out this treasure, when, in June, he prevailed upon her to cash-in her holdings to realise the sum of £200 – a large amount indeed for a working-class couple at that time. This, too, of course, was doomed. His attraction for her is unknowable: there is a physical description – a small, thin man, five foot two inches in height and weighing a little over nine stone. Cockney sparrow springs to mind, but he came from Wolverhampton!

Soon, indecently soon, on the Saturday after the wedding, Bury's violence came into the open. His landlady heard screams and found him standing over his new bride, whom he had knocked to the floor, a large knife in his hand with which he was threatening to stab her. The argument, naturally, had been about money. For the rest of their stay with her, the landlady, at Ellen's request, held the key to the Burys' door. Matters did not improve: Bury would spend all his wages on drink, and sometimes his employer's takings as well. There were regular beatings at home. In the August of 1888, they vacated their lodgings, saying that they were going to Wolverhampton. In fact, they took rooms at 11 Blackthorn Street, Bow, until December, and that, then, would have been a very famous address as Jack the Ripper's lair, if Jack he had been.

Their next home was at 3 Spanby Street, but disaster had struck – Mr Martin of Bromley had, by now, sacked his useless driver – and within a month the broken pair visited Ellen's married sister, Margaret Corney, who begged Ellen to leave her husband, but she would not. Bury told Margaret Corney that they were going away, not to Wolverhampton, but to Dundee, where he had secured jobs for both of them with a jute firm. They had no known family or friends in Scotland, and this was a drastic uprooting, or reinvention of themselves, for a couple in such humble circumstances, rather like an emigration. The decision has been thought to be mysterious, and certainly Dundee was the chief centre of the jute trade, but Bury was to make no effort to gain employment there. If he were mad, he might have entertained some delusion about Dundee.

Somehow, there was enough money left to book their passage on the steamer *Cambria*, leaving Gravesend on January 19th, to arrive in Dundee the following evening, a Sunday. They spent that night on board and disembarked on the Monday morning, with no home and no job and very little cash. They walked the cold streets, all their worldly goods humped on Bury's thin, bowed back in a large white-wood box which he had had specially made in London. Whether or not this coffin-box shows premeditation, and was always intended for a double purpose, who can say? In this guise, they obtained lodgings, late in the afternoon, with a Mrs Jane Robertson at 43 Union Street. There they stayed for only eight days, because Bury said the rent of eight shillings a week was too dear. The landlady was not sorry to see them go; she was so afraid of Bury that she would not enter his room, and asked her daughter to deal with him when he was leaving.

Bearing their box as penitents used to bear their coffins on their backs, off they went on January 29th, the rough, rootless, unlikeable couple, out of place in Dundee, to move into their new home, which Bury had already acquired by a gross cheat. Not too drunk, he had gone to estate agents in the Cowgate and enquired about two-roomed flats to let. They had given him the keys to view a basement flat under a shop in a tenement at 113 Princes Street, and he had held on to them. Now they moved in, quasi-squatters, with no intention of paying rent. Not too drunk, he had, meanwhile, turned to the Church in the hope of a handout, but the Reverend Edward John Gough, of St Paul's Episcopal Church, had been unmoved, even though Bury had brought along his bruised wife for extra sympathy. Mr Gough suggested that he should try the shipyards. Bury threw in a lie or two when the minister asked for a reference from London clergy: as it happened, although he and his wife had attended several churches, he had not made himself known to any clergyman.

The last free fortnight of Bury's life passed in a grey alcoholic haze, shot through with one crimson episode. Heaven knows how he found the money. Handy at 129 Princes Street was a public house run by Alexander Patterson, who proved friendly, and there the London misfit spent his days, a regular, slumped, out of commission. Another habitué was David Walker, a house painter, perhaps of a generous disposition, because he spent time with Bury. Back home in her bare, unfurnished rooms, with the long box a principal feature, her few personal possessions emptied out around her on the floor, cold, waiting passively for the next assault, Ellen eked out her last fortnight on earth. She made one friend of her own, Marjory Smith, who had the shop above: she naturally asked why the Burys found themselves in Dundee, and Ellen's explanation was that she had thought that the change might stop her husband's drinking. This seems unlikely to have been the real reason: it was William Bury who made all the life and death decisions in that household.

During this period, Bury acted strangely, in that he

ventured into the public gallery of the Sheriff Court at Dundee and watched the proceedings. He was surely there for a purpose, whether insane or practical. There is no innocent explanation of his desire to acquaint himself with the process of law in Scotland. He was no tourist, sightseer, or Dr Johnson, but a petty criminal soon to sink further into iniquity.

On Monday, February 4th, Bury went with a specific purpose to Mrs Janet Martin's provisions shop, a few doors along Princes Street, and bought a length of rope. 'This will do nicely, thank you,' he said as he made his selection. Night came – drinking time – and both the Burys, husband and wife, left Patterson's alehouse at closing time. Bury was drunk, and she was 'reasonably sober'.

In the early hours of the following Tuesday, the 5th, three loud screams woke up David Duncan, a 44-year-old labourer who lived at 101 Princes Street, some 20 to 30 yards away from the Burys' basement, across the communal backyard. He got up and listened for half an hour. He thought that the noises came from the Londoners' flat but he heard no more, his fire was cold and dead, and he went back to bed. From that night onwards, the blind (if there was one, or perhaps it was a part of the fittings) at the Burys' back window on to the yard stayed down.

Five drinking days passed. Bury told his friends in Patterson's that his poor wife was ill. Her name cropped up in conversation quite naturally. On Sunday the 10th, he went to see David Walker, the house-painter, and found him still in bed at noon. They chatted of this and that, and Bury picked up his friend's copy of the *People's Journal* and read out for interest a paragraph about an elopement which had ended in suicide. Walker then said, 'Look and see if there is anything about Jack the Ripper, you that knows the place.' Bury started and threw the newspaper down. Later that day, as if activated by his friend's chance remark, Bury walked into the Central Police Office in Bell Street and asked to see the officer in charge, as he had some important information. Lieutenant Parr took him into a side-room and as soon as they entered, Bury is said to have blurted out, either 'I'm Jack the Ripper!' or 'I'm a Jack the Ripper!' Never in crime could the disputed indefinite article have been of such importance. Parr failed to make any contemporaneous note but there seems to be no strong reason to repudiate the report that Bury did invoke Jack the Ripper, especially, as we shall see, in the light of a certain message on a wall, unless, to be very cautious, *that* is apocryphal.

Bury was excited, agitated and rambled as he told his story that his wife had committed suicide and he had then, like Jack the Ripper, or in his persona as the real Jack the Ripper (he did not define further) committed Ripper-ish atrocities upon her dead body. In finer detail, he went to his bed drunk, he said, and when he woke up on the following morning, he found his wife of less than a year lying dead on the floor with a rope around her neck. Then, and he could offer no explanation, it was inexplicable, he must have been out of his mind, he had no idea what came over him, he fell on her and mutilated her body with a knife. She was dead, she was dead, he hadn't killed her and now he wanted to get it all off his conscience. The body was still there in his room – it was terrible – he had squeezed it into his wooden travelling box. He seemed surprised when he was detained.

Lieutenant David Lamb, head of CID, proceeded to Princes Street, incredulous, no doubt, but bound to make investigation. The large wooden box loomed in the empty back room. Two boards on the top were loose. He prised them open and saw within a layer of bedclothes. Underneath were female legs and feet. The police surgeon, Dr Templeman, was called out urgently, and he found that the naked body was lying on its back, doubled up. The legs were folded and the right leg was broken. There were a large number of cuts and slashes across the abdomen and one at least was very deep because there was an extrusion of viscera. The neck was bruised and a piece of 'cord', with hair caught in it, was found in the room and also a bloodstained knife, with little attempt at concealment. Small fragments of what seemed to be burned cloth (never explained) were recovered from ashes in the grate.

The remains of Ellen Bury were removed to the mortuary for post-mortem, at which, quite probably photographs, now long since lost, were taken. We come now, as promised, to the writing on the wall, which still brings with it a sort of resonance of terror if we pause to think about it. Euan MacPherson has the exact location: 'There was a back entrance to the tenement block which comprised a stairway and an old door, and on that door Lieutenant Lamb found the words JACK THE RIPPER IS AT THE BACK OF THIS DOOR. At the turn of the stair, (also?) in chalk, was a further message JACK THE RIPPER IS IN THIS SELLAR.

Now, either William Bury wrote these words, or someone else did so. It is well known that Jack the Ripper graffiti appeared all over the kingdom and beyond. However, the coincidence that some daft scribbler chose the exact spot where a rippering had been done or was to be done (for we do not know how long the writing had been there) is hard to swallow. Bury *could* read and write. The strongest possibility is that he wrote the words himself, and about himself, as a perceived other person, in a very frightening, insane outburst. There is no point in saying that it is a hoax on his part, when a real woman lay dead and mutilated behind the old dark door. It *is* possible that, although his befuddled mind had not worked it out properly, he was trying to suggest that Jack the Ripper, not he, had committed the murder.

On March 28th 1889, William Henry Bury was put up at the Dundee Circuit Court before Lord Young. He pleaded Not Guilty, still adhering to his ludicrous story of his wife's suicide. Insanity was not pleaded and it would have been a hopeless endeavour in that climate. The Crown produced a peculiar forgery, the work of the accused, which purported to be a contract between him and Malcolm Ogilvy and Co., merchants of Dundee, its terms stating that Bury was to be employed for seven years at £2 per week, and his wife, if she so wished, for £1 per week. It is not divulged for whose eyes this paper was intended.

Dr Templeman gave his version of the sequence of the attack on Ellen Bury. A blow on the side of the head, as evidenced by bruising, was severe enough to have caused a loss of consciousness. She was stabbed and mutilated *before* dying from strangulation by the rope. For the defence, two doctors argued that the strangulation was of a suicidal nature and that the wounds had been inflicted *after* death. One hapless doctor, named Kinnear, admitted during cross-examination that he was of only five months' qualification, and had never seen or heard of a case of suicide by strangulation! (*Taylor:* 'This method of suicide must be regarded as of rare occurrence, but there is no doubt that it is quite possible to strangle oneself by means of a ligature.')

The jury convicted unanimously, but added an unexpected recommendation to mercy. Lord Young enquired the grounds, wondering, perhaps, if they agonised about Bury's mental state, and the foreman, (flustered, perhaps) replied that it was due to the conflicting medical evidence. Fierce, now, the judge refused to accept the rider, and sent the jury back until they returned with a plain verdict of Guilty. It was that same Reverend Gough, who had turned him away, who chose, or was chosen, to minister to Bury in the condemned cell. A reprieve failed, and Bury wept for hours. On the appointed day, he rose at 5.00am, ate his breakfast, and lit a cigarette. 'This is my last morning on earth,' he addressed a warder. 'I freely forgive all who gave false evidence against me.' The Reverend Gough, according to the newspapers, revealed, as he left the prison after the execution, on April 24th 1889, that Bury had left a written confession in which he admitted that he had killed his wife and then mutilated her body. He was not going to admit to mutilating her first, was he?

It is stated in the *Scots Black Kalendar* that Bury made a detailed confession and it or a supplementary document (it is not clear which) was forwarded to the Home Office, and that it contained some startling revelations on the Whitechapel murders, never made public. Additionally, 'He was well known in the East End of London, and several of his landlords gave him a bad character, while bloodstains were found in his rooms.' How like a much more famous 'Lodger' of bad character, Dr Forbes Winslow's candidate for Jack the Ripper, the nocturnal G Wentworth Bell Smith, given to hanging his bloodstained shirts on the towel-horse!

Although told about the crime, Scotland Yard, inundated with information about Jack the Ripper suspects, showed no interest, and no officer travelled to Dundee to interview William Bury. It had been suggested in the *New York Times* of February 12th 1889, that Bury was a likely Ripper who had murdered his wife because she suspected his identity. Donald Fraser (who does not believe that Bury was Jack the Ripper) finds that neither the 'confession' nor the 'writing on the wall' were mentioned at the trial.

Theoretically, there is no reason why Jack the Ripper, if a married man, supposing that he had not lost the taste for slaughter, left the country, committed suicide, or been placed in an asylum, should not have turned on his own wife in his own home. Killing Mary Jane Kelly in her room at Miller's Court might not have been the apogee of his animus against women. The difference in *modus operandi* (for the real Ripper, having, it is thought, strangled his victim, always cut the throat) could be explained along the lines that you would approach your unsuspecting (or even suspecting) wife in a different way from a prostitute in a dark alley. But it still does not feel right.

CHAPTER 17
THE QUEST FOR NORAH

When my husband, Richard, (delving into the rows of books which spread like the rhizomorphs of the dreaded honey fungus along the corridors of our house) first drew my attention to the Farnario case – as appeared to be the spelling of the name – I was surprised to find that there was no single book devoted to so interesting and promising a mystery. I also could not understand why it was not better known outside Scotland.

The locus was the island of Iona (or Icolmkill) in the Inner Hebrides, and I remembered seeing a television programme which celebrated its numinous, and, yes, luminous atmosphere, a sacred place to which the spiritually seeking young, especially, are drawn, and where some older in-comers have settled, unable to leave, rooted in a sense of purity and meaning in life.

My first source was Alisdair Marshall's *Scottish Murder Stories*. On the front cover, in strong black and white, there is a drawing of a young woman lying dead on a moor. Her hair streams back on-end from her brow and her face is frozen in a mask of fear. Her dark robe is decorated with pentagrams and planets. One hand is clenched in a death rigor, the other grips a long-bladed knife. In the background, a couple of crofters and a collie dog, with sticks for searching, are walking away towards a level bay and seagulls. They have not yet found her.

The facts which I gleaned from Alisdair Marshall's splendid, colourful essay, entitled *Psychic Murder?*, were that in the autumn of 1929 (his 1928 must, I think, be a misprint) an eccentric woman, named Norah Emily Farnario, came to Iona, where she boarded on a croft. The island was at that time exceptionally isolated, two days' travelling from Glasgow, with no roads, electricity, running water, daily papers, radio or telephone, but she wanted peace and serenity. Her home was in London, she was unmarried, aged 33, the daughter of an Italian academic and an English gentlewoman. In her appearance, she was singular and exotic, deliberately not in fashion, her hair worn in two long plaits, and her clothing Bohemian, arty-crafty, hand-woven in vivid dyes. Hair was raven-black and eyes were deep and intense.

On Iona she was thought (at first, perhaps) to spend most of her time writing poetry, but in London she had been involved in spiritualism, theosophy, thought-reading and faith healing. More importantly, she had been a member of the Alpha and Omega occult group, and had been an associate of Mrs Mathers, medium and sister of the philosopher, Henri Bergson. Samuel Liddell Mathers, husband of Mrs Mathers, was a leading light of another group, the Hermetic Order of the Golden Dawn.

Her hosts on the croft naturally found her somewhat strange. She spoke of visions, spiritual healing and messages from the spirit world. At night she kept two oil lamps alight in her room, but they did not prevent the ornate silver jewellery which she wore all the time from mysteriously turning black. She liked to roam the island on her own and her favourite hidden place was a marshy spot surrounded by steep rocks, thought to be the site of a pre-Christian village. Here, with the spirits of the dead, she spent many lonely hours, apparently impervious to the chills of autumn.

As the weeks went by, her behaviour changed insidiously, with agitation, anxiety, and disjointed, rapid speech, sometimes incoherent. She told her hosts not to be alarmed if she went into a trance, even if it lasted for as long as a week. She was not to be disturbed if that should happen and they were on no account to call a doctor. Not an early riser, a creature of the night, one morning she put in an appearance just before dawn and the crofters noticed the unusual pallor of her face and the way in which her hair, not plaited, lay loose in disarray on her shoulders.

Hysterically, she told them that she had to leave the island immediately. Rambling, she spoke of a rudderless ship that went across the sky. Although they explained carefully to her that it was quite impossible to leave Iona because it was Sunday and the ferry did not run on the Sabbath, she packed up all her belongings in a great hurry and made her way to the landing place. There she stood, a forlorn figure, surrounded by her baggage, gazing out across the Sound towards Mull as if willing a boat – any boat – to appear and take her off. None came and she dragged herself back to the croft, a picture of dejection, and locked herself in her room. (That was when, perhaps, with hindsight, they should have sent for a doctor.)

After a few hours, she emerged, and she seemed to have aged by years, but to have become resigned, passive. She talked quite normally, and perhaps she ate something before going off to bed, but when they knocked at her door the next morning, they found that she had vanished. Whether her bed showed that she had slept at all is not recorded, but her clothing and jewellery were in a neat pile at the bedside. The crofters raised the alarm when she had not returned by noon, and the islanders joined in a search until the light failed early in the evening. (The island covers about 2,000 acres and is rocky on the west coast, which explains the difficulty. Norah's special hideaway was presumably the first place they went to, but she was not there.)

The night was apparently bitterly cold and the frosted island was bathed in moonlight. At dawn, the search party was out again with sticks and dogs and it was a collie that found her. It barked until they drew close and its hackles must have bristled. She was two miles from the village (which may mean two miles from the croft where she lodged) in a desolate area of peat-bogs. Her body lay spread-eagled on the heather, naked except for a long black cloak with occult insignia, and a black-tarnished silver chain around her neck. Her face was frozen in a rictus of terror. It looked as if she had been running away from something, because the skin of her toes and the balls of her feet were torn, but her heels were unhurt. A long, steel knife was clenched in her hand, and her fingers had to be prised open to take it away. Underneath her body they found the rough outline of a cross gouged out in the turf by the knife. Later, there were reports of blue lights in the area, and there were rumours of a man in a cloak and a sighting of the dead woman on the day when she disappeared.

This, then, was the remarkable scenario and I thought of the stories of MR James and the idea of something that whistled coming at her across the moors. I also wondered how much contemporary journalists had embellished and improved the details of the death scene, and it was obvious that Alisdair Marshall had had his own doubts. Continuing with his account, a doctor gave heart-failure as the cause of the sudden death, although he did state that he had never seen circumstances remotely like it before.

Round about this time, over the dinner table, I mentioned the case to our doctor friend, and, off the top of his head, he suggested poison, but, to my shame, I could not tell him if there had been a chemical analysis of the organs, and I was not even at all sure that there had been a post-mortem! He told me further, that a sound diagnosis of heart-failure cannot be based on external observation alone. I did know that there is no coroner in Scottish law, and that the procurator fiscal for the district, if not satisfied with the findings of the doctor called to the scene, would have ordered a post-mortem.

The crofters built a small cairn on the spot where the body had lain and in due course a modest memorial was placed in Iona's Reilig Odhrain burial-ground among the carved tombstones of old kings, Scottish, Irish and Norwegian: made of white marble in the shape of a small, open book it bore (and surely still bears) the inscription:

I could not make out if this was a plain memorial merely commemorating the event or an actual tombstone. If the former, then the implication was that relatives had claimed her body. I was a little concerned about the date – Died 19th November – because, by reference to my reckoning calendar, I saw that the 19th was a Tuesday but the inference from the available account was that death had occurred on the Monday night, even if the body had not been found until the Tuesday.

In his discussion, Alisdair Marshall went on to say that the world of the occult was in ferment and 'psychic murder' was mooted. A leading figure, Dion Fortune, pointed out that the body had been badly scratched (but was this so?) and that the aforesaid Mrs Mathers had been linked to known cases of 'astral attacks', the victims of which always bore scratch marks. Marshall had previously noted that a 'current of will' was supposed to make an offender against the Golden Dawn's oaths of silence, secrecy and loyalty fall dead or paralysed, as if blasted by lightning.

By now, without making any great claims for originality, I was beginning to see Norah Farnario's mental state as the key to the mystery. I could not help wondering if she had a history of mental illness as suggested by the flight to the island, strange behaviour, and withdrawal from society. On the other hand you might say that she was a typical, archetypal hippy, festooned in beads, drawn to nature, although really from a sophisticated metropolitan background. Even so, as she became increasingly incoherent she could have been entering into an acute attack of paranoid schizophrenia, perhaps not her first such illness.

I think we must accept, however, that a person accustomed to rituals and spells designed to raise up spirits might reduce herself to a state of terror not associated with the disordered thinking, delusions and hallucinations of actual madness. There is a whole literature attached to the connection between psychic beliefs and insanity. In the 1870s, Dr Forbes Winslow caused consternation by claiming that 10,000 lunatics were held in American asylums as a direct result of their dabblings in psychic matters. This figure was found to be entirely false, and the doctor spent the rest of his life eating his hat!

Turning now to Richard Wilson's *Scotland's Unsolved Mysteries of the Twentieth Century* (Robert Hale, 1989) I was impressed and delighted to find that he had managed to interview Calum Cameron, then in his seventies, the son of the crofters with whom Norah had boarded, and still living, apparently in the same cottage with its four dormer windows looking out over a sandy inlet. He was twelve years old at the time, a good age for the preservation of memories. As is quite usual when there has been a mysterious death in remote surroundings – how much more so on a holy island – the local inhabitants resist our need for myth-making and pooh-pooh our suggestions that there must be more to it. Turning his weather-beaten face away from the questioner and 'looking to the heavens in exasperation', Cameron was out to deny and minimise. It was just an ordinary kitchen-knife, harmless, and there was no cross carved in the turf. 'She was just digging in the ground, maybe trying to get to the fairies inside. She was a disturbed woman, that's all. And she died of exposure as the doctor said.' I was reminded of an expedition to Lower Quinton, Warwickshire in the early 1960s, when my husband and I were received with caution and our questions about the death of Charles Walton on Meon Hill in 1945 were parried with practised incredulity. His body had been pinned to the earth by the prongs of a hay-fork and black magic had always attached to the case.

However, Richard Wilson's interviewing and research made a substantial contribution: Norah's father was an Italian *doctor*, and when she first came to Iona (he too says in 1928) she was *not* alone, but accompanied by an unnamed woman friend, who did not stay. Her motivation for the pilgrimage to Iona was her belief that she had been there in a *previous reincarnation*. She had *two* lodgings on the island: first, with her friend, she stayed with a Mrs Macdonald, and then when she was on her own, she moved away to Traighmor, the more isolated Cameron croft about half a mile from the village. She was often seen sitting down by the shore, writing. By night, she went out on lonely walks to study the mounds and stones. 'She seemed, almost, to be asking for trouble.' Her favourite haunt was, in fact, Fairy Hill, a large green mystic mound. Here, Richard Wilson's admirable historical research brought up the story of a prying monk who witnessed St Columba in communion with angels – 'Clad in white garments, they came flying to him with wonderful speed and stood around the holy man as he prayed.'

A housekeeper, Miss Varney, was traced after the death, to the 'family home' at Mortlake Road, Kew. Two days before that death, she had received a note from her mistress in Iona, which read 'My dear Miss Varney, Do not be surprised if you do not hear from me for a very long time. I have a terrible healing case on.' The housekeeper further said that her mistress used to 'moan and cry out piteously' if prevented from healing a person whom she thought she could cure. Sometimes she went off into trances for several hours, and once she embarked on a 40-day fast, but was persuaded to give up after a fortnight. She had no time for orthodox medicine – possibly because of some difference with her father, Wilson suggests.

As the strange lodger became more agitated and incoherent, she did not draw her curtains because she believed that she could see the faces of previous patients of hers in the clouds. She would write voluminously (nonsense?) by the light of the two oil lamps far into the night and be so exhausted by dawn that she would go to bed for the rest of the day. The Camerons *did* want to call a doctor but she would not let them. Some of the villagers were sympathetic and thought she had a 'persecution complex' but, says Wilson, some of their guesses 'were, and still are, less than respectful.' (Interesting.)

Calum Cameron had some good recollections of Norah's last Sunday and Monday. 'She was a'right on the Sunday night', but when his sister took up breakfast to her room there was a smell of burning, and the grate was filled with burned papers and pamphlets. The oil lamps near her typewriter were still alight. The bedclothes were 'turned down from the pillows.' Nothing appeared to be missing. *All* her clothing was still there and her watch, rings and hairpins lay neatly on the dressing-table. The Camerons *immediately* searched the neighbourhood and 'whistled for her along the shore'. After Monday's fruitless search, on the Tuesday, the police on Mull were involved.

Richard Wilson quotes from the *Glasgow Bulletin* a report which describes the body as lying in a sleeping posture on the *right side*, the head resting on the right hand. A knife was found a few feet away. There were *a few scratches* on the feet, caused by walking over the rough ground. Otherwise, there were no marks on the body. (Whether or not the body was naked is not clear, from this report, but there is such an implication in Wilson's narrative.) The *Bulletin* states that 'The doctor who was called gave it as his opinion that death was due to exposure.' The *Oban Times* states that 'Her body, which was unclothed, was discovered lying on a large cross which had been cut out of the turf, apparently with a knife which was lying by...'

Wilson's findings were that Norah was interred three days after being found, in the graveyard at St Odhrain's chapel in the grounds of Iona Abbey. Therefore, the small open book memorial does mark a real grave. Through a reading of some papers found in her room, an uncle and aunt (with no mention of parents) were contacted in London but no relative was able to undertake the journey to the island, and a solicitor was sent up to make the necessary arrangements, very much as in a Sherlock Holmes story. 'Practically every soul on Iona attended her impressive funeral'. (A post-mortem was seeming even more unlikely, although the doctor could have made an investigation in some shed on the island. I did not know how 'local' the doctor at the scene was – he *could* have come from Mull or beyond – or if another doctor was called in from Glasgow later on.)

Brian Lane's *The Murder Guide* (Robinson, 1991) was next out of the Whittington-Egan stacks (I was relieved to see that he preferred the later date of 1929 for Norah's arrival on the island – such details fret when unresolved) and I saw at once that he was most interested in the occult aspect of the case, with a knowledgeable realisation of what she had been up to in London. He asked rhetorically if she had broken some vow connected with the Alpha and Omega order, or if she had been engaged in some rivalry with an Adept more powerful than herself. He described the evolution and the history of the Golden Dawn, its infiltration by Aleister Crowley, the 'Great Beast', and a psychic struggle between Mathers and Crowley, which involved the setting on of a baying pack of 'psychic bloodhounds'.

Although she appeared to know the members of the Golden Dawn, Norah was said to be a member of an offshoot, the Alpha and Omega, where, I felt, more material about her must lie. This temple seemed to be little documented, but my husband was able to produce *The Magicians of the Golden Dawn*, by Ellic Howe (Routledge, 1972), not by any means an easy book, although very interesting. There was one reference only, to a Brodie-Innes who 'became Praemonstrator of Dr Berridge's Alpha and Omega Temple, which was under the Mathers obedience.' We appealed to our friend, Melvin Harris, author and repository of esoteric data, and he advised me to get in touch with Robert Gilbert, antiquarian bookseller of Bristol, who has himself actually published on the Golden Dawn, and he very kindly sent me some references.

The first thing that I learned was that we all had the name wrong: it should be NETTA FORNARIO. ('More Italian-sounding,' said my husband.) Dion Fortune, in her *Psychic Self-Defence* (1930), 'knew Miss Fornario intimately', and could say that she was of unusual intellectual calibre, especially interested in the Green Ray elemental contacts, 'too much interested in them for my peace of mind, and I became nervous and refused to cooperate with her...it appeared to me that "Mac" as we called her, was going into very deep waters. She had evidently been on an astral expedition from which she never returned. She was not a good subject for such experiments, for she *suffered from some defect of the pituitary body*.' Had her body, *'of poor vitality* in any case' become chilled lying thus exposed in mid-winter? (If true, and it is vague, this is a revelation, an important part of her medical history, probably not known to the certifying doctor.)

Francis King, in *Ritual Magic in England* (1970), says that when Miss Netta Fornario left London in the autumn of 1929 she took with her to Iona a number of packing-cases containing enough furniture to equip a small house, and clearly intended her stay on the island to be a lengthy one. She 'hated' her father. She boarded throughout with a Mrs MacRae. (?) The body was naked 'except for the black cloak of the Hiereus (an important officer in a Golden Dawn Temple)'. Francis King thinks it certain 'that either Miss Fornario was the victim of some sort of magical attack, or, and most people will believe this to be the more probable explanation, was suffering from an acute attack of schizophrenia and believed herself subjected to such an attack.' Francis King says that Dion Fortune actually accused Mrs Mathers of the psychic murder of Netta Fornario.

However, in *Sword of Wisdom: MacGregor Mathers and the Golden Dawn* (1975), Ithell Colquhoun notes, that 'As the incidents leading to Miss Fornario's death did not take place until some 18 months after Moïna's [Mrs Mathers'] own, the charge is scarcely worth refuting. Even if the latter had been living, the scratches found on the corpse are less likely to have resulted from an attack by Moïna in the form of a monster cat, than from running naked in the dark over rough country.' The same author defines the Alpha and Omega Lodge as established by Mrs Mathers in 1919 when she returned to London after her husband's death, and the name 'Netta Fornario' is clearly listed with names of other members. It was officially closed on the outbreak of war in 1939.

Alan Richardson, in *Priestess: the Life and Magic of Dion Fortune* (1987), has new information: 'One of Dion's best friends in the late 1920s was Netta Fornario, who wrote many articles on occultism under the name Mac Tyler. Miss Fornario was something of an artist and one who (rightly) felt that Britain had gone wrong in the 7th century in choosing, at the Synod of Whitby, to follow the Pauline Christianity of Rome rather than that of Columba in Iona.'

There ended my extra, psychic material, as I might call it. I longed to discover an old painting – of faces floating in clouds, perhaps – signed N.E.F. Contemplating the notion of poisoning, it occurred to me that Netta's luggage could have held any strange substance. Thinking about hallucinogens, (and Italian women are wise about fungi) I wondered lightly if the *psilocybe* species perhaps, or the fairy toadstool, Fly Agaric, grow on Iona in November. I can take the Corvine quest no further, and offer this tentative essay to my fellow writers in the hope that one of them will go on to produce the book that is surely there and ought to be written. We rarely leave the illusory safety of our home in the hills, these days, and I have no desire to take that route over the sea to Iona.